BROKEN

A Memoir

To God, whose love and grace have shaped my journey, I am humbled and grateful. Your presence has been my guiding light, giving me strength when I faltered and hope when I doubted.

To my extraordinary family, your unwavering support has meant the world to me. Thank you for standing by my side, cheering me on, and being my rock throughout this beautiful yet challenging endeavor.

And to all the fellow travelers on the path of healing, may our stories intertwine, weaving a tapestry of resilience and renewal. May we find solace in our shared experiences and inspiration in our collective strength.

With heartfelt thanks and boundless love,

Brittany Cecilia Jo

Prologue

You're never prepared to have to physically injure yourself. It goes against every natural reaction you have. Your brain rebels, screams at you to not even consider such a thing, and you fight back. You silence those thoughts; you know you passed the opportunity to walk away a long time ago. You find comfort in pretending that you still have an ounce of control because you know it's coming.

I close my eyes; my breath catches in the fear of the impending blow. The brick slams against my kneecap, and I wince in pain. The tears burn my eyes as I struggle to keep them in. I can't cry. I don't want to appear weak. I dig deep and mentally take myself away. Seconds later, there's another blow. I wish it would stop. I wish I wasn't here. I want to run, but the desperate need I have to be loved and accepted by these people is stronger than any love I have for myself. I sink deeper inside myself and embrace the darkness as I become someone else. There is no turning back.

She's fearless, strong, brave, everything I could never be. The switch has been flipped. I remove every trace of who I truly am to become the woman I need to be. I close my eyes; my heart rate slows; everything stills; and when I open them, I am gone, hidden in the furthest depths of my soul. The girl I see now, I do not recognize. She is empty; she feels power in the pain.

The fear drives her. She feels untouchable. I like how it feels. I like her. She is ready for whatever is to come, at least that's what I thought.

Chapter One
Present

May 17, 2018, starts like any other day. My husband and I own a construction company, and my husband had left for work early that morning. I am a stay-at-home mom to our three-year-old daughter, and we are well into our morning routine of Mickey Mouse Clubhouse, cuddles, and lots of coffee. I'm blissfully unaware of the life-changing events that are unfolding in those moments.

After some cuddles, I am at the sink washing dishes when my phone rings. I see it is my husband. It's unusual for him to call me before lunch so, naturally, when I answer, the worry has already set in. Has he been in an accident? Has something happened to a loved one? No, nothing like that. There is no way to prepare myself for what he is about to tell me.

When I answer the phone, I immediately hear panic in his voice. He is speaking so frantically that I tell myself I must be hearing him wrong.

"What did you just say?"

He repeats it, telling me that my uncle's house is currently being raided by the FBI. I'm frozen in time. Unable to move, to respond. My mind races in all the different horrific directions that I know are now possible. He explains to me the ins and outs of his morning and what is transpiring, but I can no longer hear him. I'm spiraling down a hole, crashing into the dark place in my mind where these fears have lived for years, hidden away because I naively believed this day would never come.

His voice drifts further and further away. I am on a roller coaster climbing higher and higher with every memory, every moment playing through my mind. All the decisions I have ever made are now catching up to me. Those nights, the events, the fear of knowing I never should have been there, the disappointment in myself for knowing that I should have been strong enough to walk away. I am falling, crashing at the speed of light into utter darkness.

I glance at my daughter who is sitting on the couch, watching her show, innocent and unaware of what this means for her, for our family. I find it hard to stand, to take another breath. I become very hot; the room spins all around me. How could I have done this? How could I have been so stupid?

I am jolted back to reality by my husband's voice growing louder and louder. Calling me back to my kitchen, back to my body.

"Hello? Hello!" My husband's screaming.

"Yes, I'm here."

His next sentence sends any calmness or rationality I am trying to muster right down the spiral of hell I just came from.

"You need to leave, get out of the house now. They're probably coming for you next." Sheer panic sets in. He tells me to hurry, to grab whatever I need. "Do it quickly. You don't have much time," he says.

We agree to meet at a mutual friend's house, where it will be safe. He's already on his way there, and when I arrive, when we know we are safe—at least for a while—we will try to figure out what to do next.

I hang up the phone and try my best to hold back the tears that are threatening to escape my eyes at any moment. I'm in shock and completely frightened. *What is happening? Is this it?* I have no idea how I am going to get out of this one.

I open the blinds and check outside, looking to see if I see anyone. It is quiet, for now.

I begin to scramble, grabbing things I think I might need, not sure what those things even are. I have to get out—and fast. I pick up my daughter, wrap her in a blanket, and, holding her so tight, take one final look around at our home. All of the laughter and memories we have built there ricocheting off the walls, hitting me with all their force straight into my heart.

We then leave our home, not knowing when or if we will ever be there again. As a mother, the moment I hear the slam of the door is so significant to me; it feels like the end. The end of who I am, the end of my family, of all our hopes and dreams, all destroyed in less time than it takes to order your favorite coffee. It is all crumbling around me, and I have no idea how to fix it.

Chapter Two
Present

The drive is agonizing, forty-five minutes of torture. The emotions I experience are unstable and running a million miles a minute. I am shaking, trying to focus on driving, focus on breathing. With every passing mile, I don't think I am going to make it. My thoughts jump from one bad scenario to another. I wonder if they are coming for me. Will I even make it without being stopped? I keep looking in my rear-view mirror at my sweet baby girl who is laughing and playing, wanting me to sing, "Twinkle, Twinkle Little Star" with her. Innocent, having no idea what her mother has done and how the repercussions of my poor decisions that began so long ago have just altered the whole direction of her life.

Oh, baby girl, how can I possibly sing when all I want to do is cry? How could I have let you down like this? I hope you know how much I love you.

The grief and disappointment I feel are overwhelming. I don't even want to look at myself. I don't want to look at her. What kind of mother am I? How can she ever forgive me for this?

I am in a high state of paranoia as I make the drive, eyeing every car that passes me, every car that drives behind me, scared that they will be looking for me.

Thankfully, I arrive at our meeting place without incident and see my husband standing outside waiting for me. I jump out of the car, running as fast as my legs will carry me, directly into the safety of his loving arms.

***

My husband is my best friend. He is strong but gentle, stern but playful, and hard but fair. In his arms, I always feel like nothing can get to me, like no matter, he will always protect me. So, in his embrace, I let go. I let the tears I have been holding captive finally fall. I cry and cry. Neither one of us says anything while he holds me. There is nothing we *can* say. Both of us know our lives are never going to be the same. After a few minutes, I am able to pull myself together, and my husband begins to tell me exactly what happened that morning.

Some could say the timing of the events had him in the wrong place at the wrong time, but I say it was the right place at the right time. Maybe looking back now, it was God showing up again and again, me not paying any attention. He doesn't promise bad things won't happen to you, but He does promise He will walk through them with you.

We never would have known what was transpiring if one of my husband's choices would have been different that day. That's how life is, isn't it? From the time you wake up, every decision you make sets the course for your day. Would you have been in that wreck if you had left your location any later? Would you have been caught in that storm if your plans hadn't changed? God is in control of everything, and this would not be the last time I would look back and see His grace in all of this. At this time, though, God and I weren't talking; well, He was talking, but I wasn't listening. There was no room for Him in my life as far as I was concerned, so it wasn't until much later in my story that my eyes would be opened, and I would see that He had been there all along.

***

My husband had been working at my Uncle Julian's house on a building project that was at a break point, which meant he was going to be moving to a different project for a while, so he needed to pick up his work trailer from his house. It was still a little early by my uncle's standards, so he decided to stop for breakfast first. After breakfast, he headed to the house. As he turned down the street, he noticed several black SUVs parked along the side of the road. This seemed weird, but then again, Julian had different cars around his house all the time. He pulled into the gate and proceeded down the long driveway only to find multiple unmarked SUVs everywhere and bulletproof vests on the ground that had FBI written on them. He looked around, but no one was in sight. He decided it was best to move quickly and attempt to get his trailer and get out of there as quickly as he could.

He hooked up to his trailer without incident and was about to pull through the gate to leave when he was flagged to stop by a man wearing one of the FBI vests. He slowed to a stop, rolling down his window. The man introduced himself and began to ask him a series of questions. My husband answered them one by one, putting the pieces together of what was happening. The agent informed my husband that he was free to go for now, but they would be in touch as we were on their "list".

As I am listening to all of this, I know it's bad. We are on a list. What kind of list? Are they at our house now? Are they looking for me? I don't know what is going to come next, but I know it isn't going to be good.

My husband and I sit and talk for a while about what we should do. Are we going to head home, lay low somewhere for a while? I can't help but wonder what is going on over at my uncle's house. Has he and my aunt been arrested? What did they find in the house? We are powerless to do anything, so we ultimately decide to go home. We have no idea what we are going home to, but what choice do we have? Has our house been raided? Is everyone in the neighborhood talking? Do they know what I had done?

I can just picture them all crowding the street, standing there, watching my life imploding, forming their opinions of what they thought they knew. My anxiety reaches new heights; I have never felt so afraid and so vulnerable.

I follow my husband home, my stomach turning with every passing mile. The closer we get, the sicker I feel. As we turn the corner on our street, I brace myself for the worst, but when we arrive home, to our surprise, all is eerily quiet. No commotion, no signs that anyone has been there, and no neighbors crowding around our house. There is nothing. It appears normal; you never would have known my life is imploding. For this moment, at least, we remain the nice couple on the street with the sweet little girl. Our secrets are still secrets. We know only time will tell how long that will continue.

Holding our daughter, a little extra tight, we go inside. I lay my daughter down in her crib, and sleep finds her easily. My husband and I aren't so lucky.

As we lay in bed, I wonder if I will ever sleep again. How can I sleep when I am afraid at any moment the FBI is going to show up, lights and guns blazing? Banging on my door or even busting it in? Not knowing what is happening made it impossible for me to calm myself. I lay there wide-awake, staring at the window, waiting, and listening for any sound that would alert me that they were here. Maybe if I hear them, I can stop them from waking my daughter, to keep them from traumatizing her and do my best to soften the blow of the damage I have caused.

***

Every little noise or light shining in the window from a car driving down the street put me on edge. The fear became paralyzing. I couldn't function; I couldn't sleep. The nights were the worst. All my fears crashed into me like a freight train. Alone with my thoughts, fears, and insecurities, I was vulnerable and weak. I felt Satan working hard to convince me that all of my worst-case scenarios were going to come true and that everyone would be better off without me.

"Look what you've done. You will lose everything," he whispered to me. "You are worthless, disgusting, who could ever love you now?"

I believed everything he said to me. I felt, deep inside my soul, that he was right. It overtook me; he had won. I believed his lies, and I am ashamed to say it was not the first time I allowed Satan to rage his war against me.

Time was passing, and I spent my days frozen in fear, sadness, and guilt. I was in a deep dark hole of despair. I would spend my time sitting on our couch, staring out the window, waiting. Waiting for them to come, to take me away. I barely ate. I was physically there but not present. Day after day, nothing was happening, and it was killing me.

I drank wine to numb the pain. It didn't matter what time it was, morning or evening. I didn't want to feel the pain I felt. Every day was the same thing. Every day the same result. No one came. Was this just a nightmare? Did we imagine it all? No, that would be too good to be true. That wasn't the life I lived anymore. The hope was gone.

Time continued to pass until something finally happened.

***

The phone rings, and it is my husband. The head of the investigation called him to set up a meeting. Part of us wants him to go, if at least for nothing else than to know what is going on. How bad is it? The other part of me is afraid of the outcome. After discussing it, my husband decides to not meet with him without an attorney present. This is bigger than anything we have ever faced, and we need to be smart. We still have no idea what happened at Julian and Andrea's house. We haven't heard from them and still don't know if they have been arrested or not.

A few days later, we finally have our answer. Julian calls us, and we make plans to have dinner and discuss what happened at his house that day and where we all stand now. He had been present when the FBI raided his home, so, he was confident there weren't any cameras installed watching his property.

We were not, however, sure about our cell phones not being tapped. So, we decided In-person is best.

***

The drive to his house is nerve-wracking, to say the least. We don't know what we are walking into. Is he being watched? Are we even allowed to be there? All of these questions plague my mind. As we pull down the familiar long driveway, I can't help but let my mind wander to the memories of all the other dinners we had here, all the joyful times this house held for me. I find myself pretending it's one of those times, embracing the familiarity and the comfort it brings. The house seems the same, any traces of what had occurred there a few days earlier washed away.

As we pull up and get out of the car, their little dog greets us with happy feet and a wiggly tail as she always does. Hugs are exchanged, and that's when we know it isn't a "normal" visit at all. Julian and Andrea look stressed, exhausted, and worried. They are the ones I always feel safest with, so to see them that way is disarming for me. They always make things feel better. If they aren't worried, you know you didn't need to be either. I am not going to be getting the comfort I ache for this time.

Julian's always larger than life. He draws you into his world where everything is over the top and glamorous. He walks to the beat of his own drum and never cares what people think of him. His energy is contagious. He's special, and you want him to think you are too. He taught me when I was young what it meant to give someone your word, to hold true to your commitments, and that above all family is everything. He changed the way I thought, rewiring my brain, showing me that the world isn't just black and white. It is gray, and most people can't see it because they are confined to the box life has put them in. That confident, over-the-top man, however, is not the man standing in front of me now, and my heart slowly begins to break.

We all enter the house, making our way over to the bar where I sit in the same seat, I have all the years before. Julian, true to who he is, pours us our drinks and with our drinks in hand, we move to the living room and sit down, they begin to tell us about the day the FBI raided their home. They tell us there had been multiple raids that day, and I take a moment to thank God that my home wasn't one of them. (I know, how selfish of me. God, I didn't want anything to do with You but thank You for your protection.)

I sit there listening, shocked at the details and the craziness that is now my life. It seems like a movie you watch at the theater, and I find myself in a leading role. When his recount of the events is finished, he tells me that we are all in trouble. A lot of trouble.

Julian tells us about his theory on who and how he assumes it all went wrong, which is later confirmed.

He looks at me with sadness in his eyes as he apologizes for getting me into all of this. He tells me he didn't mean to hurt me or my family. He knows that he took advantage of me, saying he knew in his heart I never would have made the decisions I did if I didn't love him so much. Which is true. I did love him, I loved him more than I loved myself, and I would have done anything for him. I did do anything for him. After all, he is the one that taught me how important family and loyalty were. I have always sought his approval, and he knew that. I was a broken teenager when he met me, and unfortunately for me, I still am, only I am not a teenager anymore. Now, I am an adult, a mother, and a wife, and I don't feel equipped to be any of these things. I am mentally, emotionally, and spiritually broken. His words sting, cut me deep into my broken soul, but only because they are true. I sit there, frozen for the moment because I don't know what to say. I don't know how to be any other way.

As the night goes on, I start to realize that this is our goodbye dinner. I can't handle it. The tears flow as we sit at his bar for what is sure to be our last time, this little family that we are, as we tell stories of the past, memories we share, and drink our favorite cocktails. I have never felt the level of sadness that currently makes its home in my heart. I know that when we leave, I will never see them again. I don't know how to live a life without them in it.

***

We knew when things went down, he was going to be punished the most. He was the "head of the snake", as they would later refer to him. This man had been in my life at that time for seventeen years. How could I say goodbye? I was heartbroken. I sat, trying to accept that the one thing he said would never happen was happening. He always said that we were safe. I believed him. I trusted that he would protect us.

As the night came to an end, we knew we were going off to face these battles alone. Each one of us was on a different path, not knowing where they would lead. We hugged, cried, and, for the last time, pulled out of the driveway that I knew so well, leaving behind the people I never imagined not having in my corner. The drive home was silent. The air was thick with worry and fear. Crying, I tried to imagine what lay ahead of us and how we were ever going to do it alone.

Chapter Three
Present

A couple of weeks have passed since our dinner when my husband receives a subpoena to go and speak with the authorities. He is to give them any information that he has on Julian, the other parties involved, and even me. The good news is that since he is finally contacted, we are finally able to apply to get him counsel. The meeting is set.

I drive into town and stay with a friend, worrying about what would happen and feeling like I need to be close to him in case something goes wrong. At her place I pace, unable to stop. I am completely powerless, and panic settles in. Time stands still as I wait for him to call. I just need to know he is ok. I need him. Our daughter needs him.

After a couple of hours, he calls and tells me he's being classified as a witness. They're not after him, thank God. He can be called upon at any time to testify, though, but he is free to leave. All I can think about at that moment is that no matter what happens to me, our daughter will at least have him. She isn't going to lose both of her parents.

After their meeting, his attorney suggests that I get representation immediately and refers me to someone that he knows and trusts.

I call the attorney he suggests and give him a quick run-through of what is going on. He has already heard about the case, as it is the largest fraud case in the county ever. *Oh, great*, I think. He tells me it isn't going to be cheap, and unfortunately, I don't have any money. He gives me some advice and wishes me well. I am so disappointed. Things are moving and happening all around me, but I have no protection. Attorneys are being scooped up left and right by the other people in the case that have money. They can pay the retainer fees and are already ten steps ahead of me. *What am I going to be left with?*

I have heard horror stories about court-appointed attorneys, and now, one of them is going to have my life in their hands. The worst part is, I can't even put in for one yet because I still haven't been officially contacted by anyone. I just need to wait, but waiting is not something I am good at.

I try my best to go on with my normal life as much as possible, knowing that at least in this moment they aren't coming for me. Confiding in the few people in my life that know what I am up against. To the rest of the world, I continue to live my lie. I smile when it is time to smile. Wave to my neighbors. Go to parties and celebrate like my world isn't going to explode at any moment. It is exhausting. I do my best to avoid everyone and everything. I am ashamed, afraid, and completely drained. I expect things to happen as quickly as you see in the movies, but it seems that I am in for a lot of hurry-up and wait. They say, "No news is good news," but when you're dealing with what I am, that is the furthest thing from the truth.

I can't handle the stress and pressure of staying in our home any longer. I want to hide. I confess this to my husband, and we decide to pack up our travel trailer and go and stay at our friend's house. They know about our situation, and it just feels better to be surrounded by support and not have to worry for a while about when the next shoe is going to drop. I need a change of scenery. I need to escape my life.

One afternoon, I talk with my husband, and we both think it is time for me to fly home and tell my parents what is going on. It's been a little over two months since everything happened, and it isn't going to go away. I know my mom can sense something is off when we talk on the phone. I try my best to act normally, but my worries consume me. Our conversations are strained and awkward. She constantly asks me if something is wrong, and I am running out of excuses. It's time to face it head-on, and this isn't something you tell your parents over the phone.

Hey, Mom and Dad, how are you? By the way, I'm under investigation by the United States Federal Government and will most likely be going to prison for an unknown amount of time. So, what's new with you?

Yeah, that won't work. It also isn't the worst idea for me to get away. The waiting is killing me, and I am so afraid of what is going to happen that it stopped me from enjoying my life anyway. Running away for a while sounds really good.

We book tickets for my daughter and me to fly to Indiana where my parents live. I'll tell them in person. They are so excited we are coming, having no idea what I am about to tell them, and I am so nervous.

I lay in bed at night going over the conversation I will have with them in my head. Each time, the scenario is different. Do I tell them together or separately? How much detail will I give? How will they react? More fears of the unknown. I think about not telling them, just going to visit, and selfishly being the only one that will know those moments, those memories we are making, that they will most likely be our last, for how long, I don't know. It's all too much.

A couple of weeks before I'm scheduled to leave, my "target" letter arrives. Holding the envelope in my hand is surreal. You don't receive mail from the United States Department of Justice often. My heart sinks into my stomach and any irrational thought I might have that this situation will somehow go away leaves immediately. I open the envelope and read the letter inside.

Dear Brittany Cecilia Jo, *blah, blah, blah,* you are currently under investigation by the Federal Bureau of Investigation and Internal Revenue Service, Criminal Investigation, for conspiring with others to commit wire/mail fraud in violation of a slew of codes, healthcare fraud, aggravated identity theft, and money laundering. We would like to discuss these charges with you, and your prompt attention to this matter is advised.

What? I begin to panic. Aggravated identity theft? What is that? I never stole anyone's identity. What is happening? I can no longer breathe. The steps it takes to reach my door feel like an eternity in the desert without water, becoming more impossible with every motion. I keep replaying the words of the letter in my head, over and over. I didn't do those things, did I? The words scream on the paper, merging as one, my focus failing. It's all so confusing. I want to run—run and hide and try to forget it all. Breathe. I just need to breathe. This is good. I know now. It is time for action. I can finally put in for a court-appointed attorney and hopefully try and make sense of all these charges and what exactly it all means. *Oh my God. Am I going to prison? How much time will I get? Will my daughter remember me?* The harsh reality of the situation I am facing becomes very clear. I am in trouble, a lot of trouble.

I go straight to work, submitting all the necessary paperwork with the court to be assigned representation and the outcome of that is the second time God showed up for me in this situation. The court-appointed attorney I am assigned is none other than the exact attorney I had been referred to a month earlier by my husband's attorney but couldn't afford. The guy I was told I needed. I am shocked and call him right away, honestly maybe a little smugly because I feel like, in some way, I have won. Just a month prior, he had told me he would only help me for an astronomical amount of money. And now, he is doing it, and the government is paying.

On my initial call with him as my official "attorney", he tells me in all his years in practice this type of thing has never happened before. He says I must have some angels or higher power watching out for me. This made me laugh. *There are no angels here, mister. Trust me.* I move the conversation on and update him on the events that have transpired so far and my thoughts about taking some time away to go and visit my family. He agrees it is a good idea to go and to tell my parents what is happening in person. We didn't know when I would no longer be allowed to travel, so it's important. I ask him for an update on any information he may have, and unfortunately, he wants to meet in person to discuss it but not until I get back. I don't want to wait; doesn't he know I am dying inside? The suspense is too much to take. I need to know everything, and I need to know now. He tells me not to worry and to go and enjoy my family. *Yeah right! How can I enjoy anything? My life is falling apart.* Waiting to find out how bad your life is about to blow up is not fun. I am no longer in charge of my destiny.

Chapter Four
Present

On July 27, 2018, my daughter and I arrive at the airport to fly from Washington to Indiana. We grab some French fries and head to the gate. As my daughter and I sit there waiting, munching on our fries, I look up to see the most surprising sight. Julian and Andrea are sitting diagonally from us. I am immediately filled with joy and a little panic that they are right there. Mostly joy, though. I run over to them, and coincidentally, they are on the same flight but getting off at our layover in Las Vegas, NV. I cannot believe the coincidence. We snap a picture, and I send it to my husband. He is just as surprised at the coincidence as I am.

My daughter and I sit with Andrea while Julian sits in the seat behind us. I feel so happy getting to see them again. We catch up on what our lives have been like the past couple of months, it feels good. It is the happiest I have been since all of this happened.

I talk to Andrea about flying home to tell my parents the news, and she gives me great words of encouragement and even shares how hard it was for her to tell her mother everything and how incredibly supportive she is and that she is sure my family will be the same way. It's Andrea being Andrea and making me feel—even if it is temporary—that everything is going to be okay.

Andrea knows my history and the struggles I have with my parents, so she knows it's not going to be easy for me to tell them this news. I honestly have no idea how they are going to react. Andrea has become like a mother to me; she's been there for me every day of my life since I was seventeen years old. These old feelings of comfort and protection that I have always associated with them come flooding back, and being with them again is the first-time things feel "normal" for me since the day this all began.

Andrea and I are talking while my daughter sits in her car seat next to me when, suddenly, out of nowhere my daughter projectile vomits all over the seat in front of us and all over me. A mom's worst nightmare. Also, a fun fact, this is the day I learned my daughter suffers from motion sickness. A small blessing passed down to her from her father.

I am shocked and start to attempt to catch the vomit in my hands. To this day, I am not sure why I ever thought that was a good idea. There I sat, no change of clothes, car seat ruined. Everyone staring at us, and I am horrified. I take my crying daughter to the bathroom, strip her down, and clean her up as best I can, all the while at the same time trying to not touch the icky airplane bathroom germs. I laugh out loud now, remembering those moments and how ridiculous I must have appeared to the flight attendant. I think at one point, I had one foot on one wall and the other foot on the sink, trying to hold my daughter up over the water like Baby Simba in the *Lion King* when he is being presented to the kingdom for the first time, as I attempt to get her as clean as I can.

I return to our seats so grateful Andrea is there with a smile on her face, waiting to support me in any way I need. I don't know what I would do if she wasn't here. She's by my side, and everything is going to be fine.

I leave my daughter with her and take myself to the bathroom to see how I can salvage anything of what I am wearing. My "cleaning up" consists of me turning my shirt inside out. Not my proudest moment for sure. I rub soap anywhere my skin is showing to try and cover up the awful way I now smell. Realizing it isn't going to get any better, I go back to my seat.

***

I genuinely believe Julian and Andrea being on the flight with us that day could not have been anything else but God showing me again His never-ending love and amazing grace. I just wish at that moment I would have been able to see it.

***

The rest of the flight is, thankfully, uneventful, and we land in Las Vegas. I am faced for the second time with the impossible task of having to say goodbye to them, my heart breaking all over again. I watch as they walk away; our journeys, once again, taking us in separate directions, and immediately, I feel alone.

After a two-hour layover, we are on our way to Indiana. The next leg of our trip goes smoother, and the kindness of the strangers on the flight are amazing. A wonderful woman traveling with her kids gives me some peppermint oil to rub on my daughter's tummy, a natural way to soothe motion sickness. She offers me snacks, tissues, and understanding smiles. My daughter sleeps sprawled out across the seats most of the flight, and I am thankful for the peacefulness.

By the time we reach our destination, I am completely exhausted, defeated, and stinking of old vomit. At this point, my daughter is mostly naked, and her ruined car seat cover is stuffed in its carry bag on my back as we walk to baggage claim. My mother meets us there, and we work together to get all of our things in the truck and craft a temporary car seat cover to get us home. Throwing the stench-ridden one in the back, I secretly hope it blows away. It is 3 o'clock in the morning when we finally reach my mother's house. All I want is to sleep. I put my daughter to bed, and as she sleeps peacefully, I lay there happy that the day is finally over but wondering how I am ever going to get through this.

Chapter Five
Present

I wake up the following morning completely exhausted. A three-year-old gets up early in the morning no matter how late you go to bed. I do not have the energy to address anything with my family that day, so I continue to keep my secret. It is so hard, and I know my stress and emotions are written all over my face. I find myself constantly in moments where someone asks me what is wrong, or if I'm okay. I always give the go-to answer we all give when we think we can handle things on our own, "I'm fine. It's fine. Everything is fine."

A few days after we arrive, I know the day has finally come. I am cracking under the stress of hiding my secret, and I want nothing more than to be free of this burden.

We're all sitting outside in the sunshine, my daughter playing in the yard, and at that moment, I just blurt out, "I have something I need to tell you guys."

My mother and stepfather both look at me wide-eyed and, at the same time, ask, "What?" with panicked looks on their faces.

I tell them I am in trouble, like in federal trouble. The kind of trouble you don't ever want to be in. My mom thinks I am joking and tells me how funny I am. She starts to walk away when I start crying. Time stops, and in that moment, they both know I am serious.

I tell them about the raid and everything that happened up until that point, silence filling the air between us, and then my mom begins to cry. It breaks my heart to see her cry, to know that she is hurting because of me. I take a deep breath and tell them what my charges are and that I don't know how much trouble I am in. The conversation seems so surreal to me, as it will every time, I am faced with having to share my story with someone. It just doesn't fit, and I can't believe this is happening to me. I am not a bad person. I certainly am not a criminal. I never did anything wrong, well except for this one big thing that I struggle to understand how I ended up here myself. I question myself. *How did this happen? How did I end up here?* Well … that is a more complicated story.

Chapter Six
Past

To be honest with you, I have rationalized every reason that I could come up with on how exactly a "good, normal" girl like me ended up here, but the truth is, I've never been normal. I never lived that normal life. My childhood was filled with its own set of trials and traumas, and that is where I feel like it all began. At least that's what all the therapists say.

I grew up in a broken, toxic environment. My biological father was the first rejection I faced. For the first few years of my life, he would come and go, leaving a trail of heartache and disappointment in his path, and then one day, he was just gone for good. I don't know if he left because of my mother or because he just didn't want me. Either way, all that ever mattered to me was that he was gone. He didn't love me, didn't want me, and I wasn't good enough. Nothing makes that easier. All you are left with is a whole half of you that you don't know or understand.

Growing up, people would say, "You look so much like your father." It was always a reminder of the rejection I felt, and the worst was when my mother would say it. I always felt like she loved me less because I was her constant reminder of him. I had no connection to the last name I carried; it meant nothing to me. It only made me feel alone. There wasn't a single person in my family that shared the same last name that I had. Did I only partly belong? And if so, where *did* I belong?

When I was four years old, my mother met the man that would become my stepfather. They met in a bar, so to be fair, it shouldn't have been a surprise when his drinking and drug use became a problem. My mother had a pattern after all, and he fit the mold. The bad boy, the troublemaker, the guy you always think you can change. Deep-rooted generational ties from her mother, who probably got it from her mother, and so on. I'm sure a lot of us are personally familiar with this cycle of chaos, or you at least know someone whose picker just seems to be broken—a different guy but the same result every time.

Over the next thirteen years of my life, I was forced to endure a relentless cycle of physical, emotional, and verbal abuse at the hands of my stepfather. Time and time again, his explosive anger would manifest in violent assaults against my mother, stepbrother, and myself, forcing us to flee in the dead of night in search of safety. But just as predictably as we left, we always returned, swallowed up once more by the suffocating grip of fear and lies that Satan whispered into my mother's ear. The lies that she wasn't good enough, that she couldn't make it on her own, that she needed him.

The most devastating reason why she would always return was that my mother was madly in love with him. Her love for him was the one thing that kept her bound to him, despite the danger and pain that came with it. She loved him, and love makes you a fool.

I developed early in my youth, and that brought a lot of attention to me. The boys noticed me, and the girls hated me. I tried to hide my body by wearing baggier clothes, but that didn't seem to help either. It only made me get teased for being fat. The little self-esteem I had was dwindling more and more. The boys in the neighborhood treated my body like it belonged to them, grabbing me, or touching me whenever they wanted. It happened to all the girls on the street. Honestly, it happened so much that it seemed normal, and it would be a lie if I said the attention didn't feel nice. I was being noticed, and when you are desperate to be seen, even negative attention is still attention. It was in those days that I started placing my value in what others thought and said about me. Do what everyone else does, and you will fit in; don't make them mad, and they will like you.

When I was thirteen years old and at my lowest point, I was targeted by a few boys at my middle school who decided that I had something that they wanted, and they were going to take it. I kept to myself, and that made me seem intriguing, a challenge to be conquered.

I was at the drinking fountain during class one day, which was in a separate area from the gymnasium. It was separated by two sets of doors, one on each side of the hall, closing you off from others. It was here that they entered, securing the doors behind them. I hadn't even looked in their direction yet as the feeling that something was wrong quickly swept over me. A sinking feeling in my stomach told me to get out of there quickly. I looked at the doors, trying to figure out how I could pass the boys that now stood between me and the safety of my class, preparing myself to walk away as casually as I could.

I took my first step, and in what felt like no time at all, they were right behind me. Any sense that I was maybe exaggerating about the situation, being dramatic, quickly faded as tingles coursed through every inch of my body. It was a warning. I ignored the closeness of them, continuing in my direction toward the door when one of them stopped me.

"Where are you going?" he asked.

"Back to class," I said, as I tried to put some distance between them and me.

At this time, another boy grabbed my wrist and pulled me back. It wasn't until one of them grabbed me and slammed me against the wall that I realized I had been so focused on the door I never noticed that they were surrounding me. Panic set in. I was pinned against the wall, my arms being raised above my head, my wrists being held tightly while another began pulling up my shirt. The coldness of their hands sent shivers down my spine, and I felt sick to my stomach. They began taking turns touching my breasts, squeezing them hard, saying how big they were, that only sluts had big tits like this. I was jerking underneath them to try and get away, but nothing I did mattered. I was powerless. The strength and weight of them was too much. Fear took over me, and I was frozen. They were going to win, and there was nothing I could do to stop them.

One of the boys began to move for my gym shorts, the look on his face saying exactly what all of their intentions were. I braced myself, preparing for the worst when, by the grace of God, a teacher walked in through the door. The boys instantly released me, and I covered myself up quickly as I gave a pleading look to the teacher. My makeup smeared down my face from the tears. I waited, holding my breath, waiting for him to do something, to say something, to save me, to do anything, but all he said was "Get back to class." It felt like a gut punch. He wasn't going to do anything.

It was too much to take in, so I ran. Frightened and unable to breathe, the tears fell like rain out of my eyes. I ran down the hall, having no idea where I was going. I just needed to get as far away as possible. It seemed like I would be destined to run my whole life. I ran right into another student; a girl I knew of but wasn't close to. Who was I kidding? I wasn't close to anyone. She was looking at me, shocked, as concern spread across her face. I couldn't get the words out. I couldn't calm myself long enough to speak. Not knowing what to do, she walked me to the principal's office. I sat, waiting for him to call me in, on edge the whole time of being seen. *What would the boys do if they saw me in here? Did everyone know?* Finally, I was called back.

I hurried into the office, slamming the door behind me. I sat for a while, not saying anything, the shock and devastation of it all barreling down on me. I could feel his eyes on me. The weight of his stare intensified the shame I had brewing inside of me. After a few minutes that felt like hours, I began to tell him what had happened, each word I said out loud chipping a little more of my self-worth away. He listened and told me he would be looking into the incident and would decide the best course of action. I chose to spend the remainder of the day in the office until, finally, the last bell rang, and I was free.

I couldn't get onto my bus quickly enough. I sat on the bus, trying to make myself as invisible as possible. I felt nothing but dread. I had no idea what was going to happen now that I told, and worse, what nightmare did I just open myself up to. I felt ashamed. Dirty. Like a piece of garbage. I felt like someone that no one cared about, and they never would.

When I arrived home, the tears once again got the best of me as I told my mother of the incident, and to my horror, she didn't believe me. How does your mother not believe you when you come home and tell them something so awful has happened to you? That was it.

I felt it the moment it happened. My soul, the very essence of my being, shattered into a million pieces, and I knew I had nothing left. I had fought all I could fight. Even my mother didn't love me enough to believe me. I was broken, and there wasn't anything that was going to put me back together. So, I ran. I ran out of the house and headed down the street. I ran until I couldn't run anymore, and my lungs felt like they were going to explode out of my chest. I collapsed in a patch of grass, staring up at the sky, watching the birds fly by. I wished I was a bird. I wanted nothing more than to fly away, to be free of my life. I don't know how long I laid there. I could see the colors of the sky begin to change and knew I needed to go home.

Upon my return, my mother told me the principal had called to discuss the incident with her and validated everything I had said. She tried to hug me and apologize for doubting me, but at that point, the damage was done. I had no reason to carry on. I went to my room, and that night, as I cried out all the pain, the hurt, and sadness, I took a razor blade to my wrist. I watched the blood pour out as an uneasy calmness filled me. I didn't want to die. I knew that. It was a desperate attempt to be seen, to feel loved, for someone to care. It was the only thing I thought at that moment to do.

Well, the response from my "parents" had the opposite effect. They decided I was unstable and needed to be sent off to a mental hospital for troubled teens for the summer. They were going to throw me away like trash, just like everybody else. The weird thing is, I wasn't even mad about it. I was happy to be away from them, from everything.

I arrived at the facility and didn't even acknowledge them. I was done. I think the staff could sense the tension because we were separated pretty quickly, which I was grateful for. I didn't want to say goodbye. Sometime after I arrived, my stepbrother showed up and was admitted. I guess my parents felt like he was a burden as well. It was comforting having him there with me. We were a team and slowly began to tell people about the life we had been living. The fights, the emotional and physical abuse we had all endured from my stepfather, and slowly, I grew to like it there. I met kids like me that went through some of what I went through. They understood me. I belonged somewhere.

The counselors listened to us and supported us. We had never been able to get any sort of counseling growing up because as soon as anyone would begin to question my parents, there would be a big scene, and we would be pulled out immediately, never to return. I don't know how many counselors met us throughout the years, and we never got to finish our treatment.

Unfortunately, the same thing happened at this facility when my parents were questioned about the details my brother and I had shared with the staff. My parents became upset and wanted me to be discharged immediately, and I was to return home with them. That was the last thing I wanted.

When it was time to go, I tried everything to be able to stay, even threatening to cut myself again. In my mind, it seemed like the logical thing to do, commit the same act that got me put there in the first place, but as with most things in life, it did not bring the desired outcome, at least not exactly. I didn't have to go home with my parents, but I didn't get to stay there either. Nope. They moved me to a more secure facility, one that was not as friendly or supportive, and after a month of misery, I ended up returning home where I found out my brother had been sent to live with our grandparents in Florida. I was so jealous he was free.

I laid low when I returned home and was enrolled in a different school. I was too scared and ashamed to ever go back and face my attackers, and it seemed I wasn't welcome back either. That was fine by me. I buckled down, going through the motions of the life that I seemed trapped in. I was used to being the new girl. I played the part well. It was fun because I was able to recreate myself each time. I could be anyone I wanted to be. I knew I wouldn't be anywhere long anyway; my parents were my parents after all.

There were more "incidents" that were followed by four more moves which brought five new schools with them. By this time, I was in survival mode, doing nothing but existing every day, waiting for the opportunity to escape, to leave it all behind once and for all. To run.

At seventeen years old, that time finally came, and I took it. I ran. I ran away from the abuse, from the fear, the sadness, the emptiness of it all. I ran away from being the protector of my siblings and my mother. I ran away to finally put myself first, wanting nothing more than to fight as hard as I could to break the cycle I seemed destined to repeat. I ended up running straight into the arms of a guy that I should have realized was too good to be true. Anchoring myself to him would set the course of my life straight to the nightmare I currently found myself in.

Chapter Seven
Past

It was July 2002 when I met Richard for the first time. I was vacationing in Las Vegas, NV, visiting my aunt for the summer. I looked forward to visiting her whenever my parents would allow. She was a safe place where I could go and just be me. I was able to set aside my "normal" life when I was with her. There was no drama, no yelling, and no fear of not measuring up. We were looking forward to me starting my senior year of high school, graduating, and the freedom that college would finally bring me to set off on my own and conquer all of my dreams.

One night, while I was visiting, she told me she had a work friend coming over, and she would be bringing her son. I didn't think much of it at the moment, a setup from my aunt with someone's son was the furthest thing from my mind. My life was too complicated to entertain a summer romance that would ultimately end up going nowhere, and one of us would just end up hurt in the end.

When her friend arrived, she was solo, and I was relieved. I assumed he felt the same way about the situation that I did and made the smart decision to bail. I was wrong. Turned out, he had decided to drive himself, and he would be arriving shortly. I learned later in the evening it was in case he was not "feeling it".

The sun was beginning to set, and we were all visiting in the backyard when a tall and slender figure appeared from around the corner of the house. I raised my eyes, trying not to make it obvious that I noticed him, and I think I stopped breathing.

He was unlike anyone I had ever met. He was two years older than me but seemed so grown up. He was straight out of every fairy tale story I had ever been told—the prince charming that comes to save you from every bad thing in the world. I fell for him instantly. He was handsome, wore a suit, had a job, had a nice car, and, of course, was sweet, charming, and romantic. He was everything that now would scream at me, *too good to be true*, but at seventeen, that thought never crossed my mind.

We sat around that night talking for hours, learning all there was to know about each other. I fell deeper and deeper as every moment passed. The night was coming to an end, and neither one of us wanted to be separated. He asked to take me for ice cream, but my aunt said no. At the time, I was furious but soon discovered it was the right choice.

"Leave them wanting more," she said.

It worked. He called me almost immediately and asked me out to dinner the very next night. I had never been taken out to dinner. It was all so magical, so unlike anything in my life. We spent the rest of my trip inseparable, falling more and more in love with each other. I was the happiest I had ever been in my life. The time came for me to go home, and I was devastated. How was I going to leave him?

We promised to talk on the phone every day and began making plans for me to return for my Christmas break. It was only four months away. We could do it for four months, and we did. With each call, I grew more in love with him. He was the best thing in my life. I dreaded going home every day but knowing I would get to talk to him got me through.

Christmas break finally came, and I had butterflies in my stomach when I thought of seeing him again. My flight landed, and the anticipation of our reunion was electric. My nerves were in full force. Would we be the same? Would he see me and still want me? All my insecurities hit at once. Who was I to think I was good enough for someone like him? Why would he choose me? No one else ever had.

I had had boyfriends before, of course, but none that I let myself care more for than they cared for me. I had to be in control. I kept them at a distance to protect myself. You weren't going to hurt me; I would hurt you first. I always left them when I felt they were beginning to care too much, or if I thought I could actually care for them one day, the alarms in my heart would start blaring in my head and I would know it was time to end it. Now, I realize that sounds cruel. It wasn't that I didn't like them or was unkind to them in any way. I just had to protect myself, and in the end, I believed I was protecting them too. Unfortunately for me, when it came to Richard, I lost all of that power. He had completely disarmed me in a matter of minutes when we met, crashing straight through my heart and leaving me defenseless in anything regarding him. I was madly in love with him.

I raced off the plane, trying to get to the baggage claim as quickly as I could, knowing he would be there waiting for me, and there he was, flowers in hand. My tall, dark, handsome man, and like magic, all my worries faded away. He scooped me up into his arms and kissed me just like they do in all those romantic comedy movies. Spinning me around and around as if we were the only two people that existed in the world. My heart was full, and I knew I was home.

Christmas Eve morning arrived, and I woke to someone caressing my head and whispering my name, ever so softly, urging me to wake. I opened my eyes to find Richard sitting on the edge of my bed. He told me to get dressed in warm clothes. We were in Nevada, so the request was strange. I was from Pennsylvania after all, and this weather was not cold. He leaned forward and ever so politely mentioned that I should also brush my teeth. I did as instructed, and when I emerged from my room, I was met by my aunt presenting me with a mug of hot chocolate and a bag of chocolate chip cookies.

"Have fun," she said.

I gave her a hug, and we walked out to the car. I was then blindfolded and placed in the vehicle ready for departure. We drove away, and I remained blindfolded the whole journey, which seemed like hours. He played romantic music the whole drive, and my curiosity was beyond piqued. We listened to Backstreet Boys, N*SYNC, and 98 degrees. I was a part of the boy band generation, and I loved it. I listened to the words, knowing he was speaking to me with each song he chose to play.

It seemed like we were driving really far outside of town, and after a while, the paranoia began to creep in. How well did I really know this guy? He could be a serial killer. Once, my thoughts got the best of me, and I flat-out asked him if he planned on murdering me and dumping my body wherever it was that we were going. Of course, he told me I was being ridiculous and laughed a little. *That's what they all say*, I thought to myself, and then finally, the car came to a stop.

He instructed me to wait in the vehicle with a blindfold on until his return. Although I was tempted to sneak a peek, I refrained. As time ticked by, I found myself questioning my decision to trust someone I barely knew. We had driven for some time, and no one knew my whereabouts. Worrisome scenarios flooded my mind. Was I foolish to trust him? As my anxiety escalated, I realized I needed to calm myself down. Taking a deep breath, I reminded myself that everything was fine and that I was overreacting. He was trying to be romantic. I pushed the nerves away and decided to wait patiently for his return. He went through so much trouble to make this moment perfect; I didn't want to ruin it. Whatever *it* was.

A few moments later, my door opened, and I was struck by the intensity of the cold temperature. Where were we?

"Are you ready?" he asked.

"Yes," I said.

At that moment, he removed the blindfold from my eyes, and standing in front of me were two Clydesdale horses attached to a sled. I was shocked. I began to look around and realized we were in the mountains, and there was snow everywhere. We were at Mount Charleston, a place for those that live in the constant heat of Las Vegas to go when they desire to get away and experience all the beauty winter has to offer.

We climbed up into the sled, a blanket placed across our laps, and I finally understood the need for the hot chocolate. This was the most magical moment of my life. I was getting comfortable and ready to go when, suddenly, something spooked the horses, and they started charging toward the edge of the cliff. Panic set in, and I froze. We clipped the side of a nearby parked truck. All I heard was the crunch of the sled absorbing the impact as the startled horses continued toward the edge.

"Jump! Jump!"

The screams of the sled driver came into focus as our bodies reacted, and we each jumped out of the sides of the sled. The driver was thankfully able to grab the reigns of the horses, bringing them to a halt, inches from what surely would have been their demise.

Trying to get my breathing under control, I tried to process what had just happened. Thankfully, everyone was fine. A few moments later, after the horses had calmed down, the driver approached us, apologizing and informed us they were ready to go.

"Climb on in. We're ready."

Ready? Oh no. I am not getting back into that death trap. There was no way. After ten minutes of Richard begging me to get back in, I finally conceded. We began our ride, and after a few minutes, I started to relax a bit. The horses seemed calmer, and the scenery was breathtaking.

A little while into our journey, Richard began to speak. "You know I love you, right?"

"Yes," I said.

"You mean so much to me, and I can't imagine my life without you." He pulled a small box out of nowhere, opened it, and presented me with the most beautiful ring my seventeen-year-old self had ever seen. "Will you make me the happiest guy in the world, and marry me?"

The world stopped. Now, I know I should have said it was too soon, that we needed to get to know each other better, that we were too young to think about getting married. I should have said a lot of things. Instead, with my heart exploding and tears streaming down my face, I said, "Yes."

It was the easiest question I had ever answered. I was never going to feel alone again. He loved me. Me, and I honestly believed we were going to be together forever.

There would have been no way for me to anticipate the repercussions of the decisions that were made on that day. Upon hearing the news of my engagement, my mother was less than pleased. She became incredibly angry on the phone, yelling that I better get on that plane and come home. The thought of not coming home had never crossed my mind. We were making plans for him to fly over and take me to my prom, watch me graduate, and then my eventual move out to Las Vegas, NV to be with him. I was so confused over her reaction and now, yes, frightened to return home. We enjoyed the last few days of my trip, and then I boarded the plane that would carry me to face my mother.

As expected, upon my return, my home quickly became a hostile environment. My mother and I were at odds over my choices. I was not permitted to wear my ring in the house. I was told not to speak to him. I was to forget him altogether.

School was my only refuge. Another time in my life that God was there for me, but I could not see Him. He aligned me perfectly with a few angel staff members that cared for me, helped me, counseled me, and supported me through the ups and downs of my home life. I never would have made it if it were not for them, and I will forever be grateful.

My mother and I argued daily, and the sadness, anger, and loneliness I felt consumed me. I didn't understand why she was trying to ruin the best thing in my life. The final blow, you could say, occurred about a week after I had been back.

My mother and I were fighting per usual, and things were escalating quickly. She grabbed my wallet—she knew I put my ring in it whenever I returned home, doing my best to respect their rules. Panic set in, and I knew I could not let her have it. She was going to get rid of it, and I knew if she succeeded, I would never see it again. It was not something you could just replace.

It all happened so fast, and I wish I could remember who said what, why, and all that, but it does not matter. What does matter is in the scuffle of trying with all my might to get my wallet back, my mother slapped me, and I am ashamed to say, I slapped her back. Time stood still with the sound of the crack. I grabbed my wallet and ran for my life out the front door, barefoot in the snow about ten blocks to my friend's house. I was banging on the door, hysterically crying, when it finally opened, I lunged myself into my friend's arms. We went up to her room, and I told her what happened. Her mom called my mother, and after some convincing, my mother said it was okay for me to stay there to have a cool-off period.

It was that night, in the dark, unable to sleep, that I made the decision that I had finally had enough. I could not live this way anymore. I had dreamt of running away my whole life, and it was finally time. I was seventeen, three months away from turning eighteen, and it was time to save myself. I informed some of the trusted people in my life of my decision, and the plans began to fall into place. The date was set. I would leave in two weeks, on January 30th, which would be the end of my second quarter of school.

I returned home and was on my best behavior, knowing that my freedom was coming. I began to slowly bring my most treasured possessions to school in my backpack and stored them in my locker. Every day, I added a few more items that I couldn't leave behind.

The morning to leave finally came, and I found myself struggling to say goodbye to my little brother and sister. I had cared for them and protected them their whole lives and felt a bond with them stronger than just a sibling. I grieved the loss of them as a mother would toward a child. I was abandoning them, and I knew they would never forgive me. I hugged my baby brother, knowing it would be the last time for a while, silently apologizing to him in my head. I carried the burden of knowing the truth in my heart, and it crushed me. My sister shared a room with me, and I spent that night staring at her, watching her sleep. Trying to find some way I could take her with me, knowing there wasn't one. I kissed her forehead, tucked her in tightly, and cried myself to sleep.

I awoke the next morning the same as every day, but this time, my heart shattered into a million pieces as I closed our bedroom door behind me, the tears streaming down my face. They were my hardest goodbye. I stood behind my decision to leave. I knew it was the right thing for me, but it didn't make it easier. I truly believed there had to be something more out there for me, something better. There had to be happiness somewhere. This couldn't be all there was.

I arrived at school that day like normal, knowing that everything about this day was different. I checked into homeroom just as I had planned; this would keep me off the absentee list. However, when the bell rang, instead of walking to my class like I had done hundreds of times before, I met my best friend in the hall, and together, with nothing but my backpack, we walked straight out the back doors of the school to the Lincoln Town Car waiting to drive me the two and a half hours to the airport. This was it. No turning back.

I was doing this. In a couple of hours, I would be a runaway. Not exactly how you pictured your life going.

The car left the parking lot of the school, and I twisted around to stare out the back window. I watched as everything faded away, getting smaller and smaller the further we drove until there was nothing left. More than once, I questioned my decision and my sanity, but I was certain. This was the way out, and I had to take it.

I looked out the window as the car sped down the highway. The trees passed in a blur as the tears cascaded down my face. Every emotion hit me like waves crashing into the ocean. I was seventeen years old, and I was embarking on a life-changing journey. I was breaking the law to save myself, yes, but I was still breaking the law. I was scared.

I arrived at the airport, nervous I was somehow going to be caught, like everyone knew, and they were going to send me back home, but that never happened. Everything went smoothly boarding the plane, and before I knew it, I was on my way. I passed the time by reading and listening to music, my mind consumed with both worry and excitement over what I had just done.

The time change in Las Vegas, Nevada was three hours behind Pennsylvania, so when I landed it was already late at home. I knew my mother knew something wasn't right by this time. I would have gotten home from school hours earlier, and I never showed up. I was a wreck, panicking, letting it sink in that I was now clear across the country and only a few people knew. It was the craziest thing I had ever done. I was a good kid. I never got into trouble. I didn't do things like this. I quickly started regretting my decision, mostly out of fear, but nevertheless, I was questioning it. I pushed those feelings aside, reassuring myself that I did the right thing, and I couldn't focus on my insecurities right now. Richard was waiting for me at the baggage claim, and as soon as I saw him, all my worries washed away in his embrace. I needed him. I felt safe with him. I gave everything I had to him. Whatever was left of my heart and soul, he held it all in the palm of his hands. I truly believed he was the only one that loved me, that understood me, and I knew that he would always keep me safe.

We got to the car, and after a few deep breaths, he handed me his cell phone. We had planned to call my mother upon my arrival, if nothing else but to reassure her that I was safe and nothing bad had happened to me. I was nauseated. I knew it would not go well, and I was losing the courage to stand my ground.

After a few rings, she answered. Once I told her it was me, the screaming began. I did my best to remain calm and stick to the script we had rehearsed over and over in anticipation of this very reaction. I was to inform her that I was only calling to let her know that I was safe, that I wasn't going to be returning. I needed to do this for me, and I asked her not to worry about me. As expected, she was furious, and I knew we weren't going to get anywhere right now. Emotions were too high. So, with utter sadness in my heart, I hung up.

That was the last time I spoke to my mother for seven months. Within that time, she tried everything to get me back: phoned the local police, sent officers to look for me, called Richard's cell phone at all hours of the night, screaming and cussing at him to send me home. It was a really hard time, and for our protection, I went into hiding until I turned eighteen in April. Once that day came, there wasn't anything anyone could do. I was an adult and was allowed to make my own choices. We slowly began to build a life together, and everything was wonderful, at least for a while.

Richard quickly became my sole source of happiness, my purpose. I spent my days doing housework and trying to stay busy, waiting for him to return home from work, playing the role of the dotting housewife. Some days were harder than others, though, and I wouldn't get out of bed. I was afraid to be alone. Having never been on my own, I was crippled with anxiety. I became paralyzed in fear whenever he was not around. I no longer knew where he ended, and I began. I had always lived in a small town and knew everyone around me. Now, I was in a big city filled with people unfamiliar to me, in an area I didn't know, and felt unprepared to protect myself.

I was young, naïve, and had no life experience to fall back on. Sometimes, the fear would consume me so much that I would lock myself in our bedroom until Richard would get home from work. As time went on, my fears dissipated, and I began to branch out more. I found a job, made some friends, and began to form a life of my own. I was discovering who I was and attempting to stand on my own two feet. It felt great, but this was when the fighting began.

Now, for the sake of honesty, I will tell you that I had no idea how to fight fairly. The only example I had was my mom and stepdad, and they didn't know how to fight fairly either. We were two broken people, from broken homes, thinking we could figure it all out on our own. Each one of us fought our battles the way our parents did. We would yell, cuss, name-call, and say hateful things to each other. Richard would punch holes in the walls and break down doors I'd locked to try and get away from him. My instincts to run would kick in at the first sign of violence, and I would find myself running through our apartment complex in the dark of night, looking for the closest place to hide.

One night, I spent over an hour in a bush, hiding. Once I calmed down and realized the bush was just as scary, I made my way home. The emotions of the night and the worry Richard felt not knowing where I was would take over, and he would no longer be mad. He would shower me with love and tell me how sorry he was, and I would fall into his arms. We would go back to being madly in love, promising we would do better, be better, but it never was. It seemed the more independent I became, the more we would fight. He became jealous and questioned everything I did, never wanting me to go out with my friends without him. His friends became my friends, and we were always together unless we were at work.

One night, we got into a horrible fight because someone from my past who had been my childhood best friend reached out to me. They were going to be in town and wanted to get together. He immediately got angry, accusing me of having a relationship with this person, calling me names, and telling me to just leave and go be with him since that's what I wanted to do so badly. I was heartbroken. How could he even think that? I begged him to listen to me, to trust me. I hadn't even responded, nor did I have any desire to go. He didn't believe me and locked himself in the bathroom.

This was the first time that Richard threatened to kill himself if I ever left him. I banged on the door, pleading with him to open, to let me love him, promising that I wasn't going anywhere and how sorry I was. Taking full responsibility for everything that happened, having convinced myself that I indeed had done something wrong. I found myself leaning more and more on him and less on anyone else in my life. I was convinced that without him, I would have nothing. All I arrived with was a backpack; everything else I had was from him. He owned me.

A few years into our relationship, we began to spend more time with his Uncle Julian and Aunt Andrea. They became more like parents to me, filling a void in my heart that was there all my life. We had dinners together, vacationed together, went to parties together, and quickly found ourselves engrossed in each other's lives. They were entrepreneurs and had more money than anyone I had ever known. Their houses were lavish, and their cars were cars normal people like me only dreamed of driving. And now, I found myself driving around town in Mercedes, Jaguars, and Bentleys. Everything about them was lavish, over the top, and amazing. I never questioned anything that I was told about what they did or how they made their money. All I knew was that they were in real estate and did very well for themselves. It all seemed to fit. I was young and naïve, and really, I didn't think about it much.

As time passed, it started to become clearer that they didn't just sell real estate, and I found myself invited into what they called the "circle of trust". There was only a handful of people that were trusted enough to be brought into the other side of their lives, and I was so honored that they picked me. They trusted me and valued me. I was somebody now. It made me feel good—maybe too good.

I began to learn how Julian thought, the inner workings of his brain. He was one of the smartest people I had ever met. His logic and reasoning made complete sense, opening my eyes to ways and thoughts I never would have imagined. My brain was being rewired to think the way he thought, act the way he acted. The feeling of family and trust that we all shared was like nothing I had ever experienced.

As time went on, I came to realize that I would do anything for these people. I trusted them completely, and it was that unwavering trust that would put me in the position I would soon find myself a part of at our next family meeting. The idea fell upon Julian completely by accident, but once that seed had been planted, there wasn't anyone that could change his mind. Soon, we would all know what it meant to really be in the "circle of trust".

***

Richard had been driving to work one morning when a drunk driver ran the red light and t-boned him. Thankfully, his injuries were minor, and not knowing what to do, we called Julian. He helped us walk through the process of working with the insurance company and getting our car fixed. We were learning the ins and outs of how the system worked and were shocked, when on a routine phone call with our insurance company, Julian found out the impaired driver was suing us, and our insurance company was going to settle with him for $17,000.00. We were stunned. Why should we have to pay him? He ran the red light. He had alcohol on his breath. It didn't make any sense. This was the seed planted, and the more knowledge Julian obtained, the more the seed grew until it began to spread in his mind like wildfire.

We were sitting in his basement, where we had most of our family meetings, when he presented us with his idea.

"We can do this," he said.

We all sat there looking back and forth at each other, unsure exactly what *this* was. As the realization dawned on us, it became clearer. He wanted us to stage car accidents. He had put hours, days, and weeks into his research, planning and studying. He had answers for every question and every rebuttal that was presented. He made it sound so easy, logical, and harmless. There would never be anyone involved that wasn't a part of the circle. It would be safe. No one would be around. There was no chance for a bystander to suffer at our hands for anything we did.

At the time, you would hear stories about people slamming on their brakes to make people hit them, causing financial harm and sometimes hurting a stranger to make a quick buck. That wasn't going to be us. *Is there a way to do something like this honorably?* It was completely crazy, nonsense, never in a million years. This wasn't me. I didn't commit crimes.

I heard his voice playing in my head over and over, "*We won't get caught. We're only screwing over insurance companies. They will just write it off.*

You're not harming anyone. We will only get caught if someone tells. No one here is going to talk. I will take the fall. I will take the blame, but it will never come to that."

I slowly found myself believing his words, justifying it to myself. I held onto every word like it was the truth, pushing the sinking feeling in my gut further away, rationalizing that every terrible thing I was feeling was just nerves, excitement, and adrenaline.

Richard and I drove home, and I couldn't believe that we were even entertaining the idea, let alone possibly agreeing to it. What had I gotten myself into?

The night of my first "accident", I was a wreck. Every part of my body screamed, rejecting the very idea of what I was about to do. I was so stressed out I could not stop going to the bathroom. I was becoming physically ill knowing what I needed to do, but there was no backing out. After weeks of planning and organizing, every detail already planned out, people had been recruited, and money was spent. This had to happen. They needed me and were depending on me to do what I was supposed to do.

I kept reminding myself, *You gave your word. Julian loves that about you. He would always say, "Your word was all you had."* He was the type of guy that still believed if you shook on it, it was the same as a contract. If you gave your word, that was that. I knew he felt that way, and it was a trait he admired in others. I wanted to be that for him. Loyal more than anything else. I could not let him down.

Deep breaths, Brittany. You can do this. What am I thinking? I most definitely cannot do this. I feel short of breath as I arrive at the hotel for prep. I enter the room, and the energy is buzzing with a mixture of fear, excitement, anxiousness, and nerves. Julian had assigned me my role, and all I had to do was get into character.

No one can ever truly prepare for the moment when they have to hurt themselves. It defies every instinct and impulse in your body. Your mind screams at you to stop, to turn away, but you know you can't. You've come too far, made too many choices that led you down this path.

So, you steel yourself, try to regain some resemblance of control. It's all you have left. I close my eyes, bracing myself for the impact, the inevitable pain that I know is coming. I don't feel it at first; it's the sound of the crack of the brick hitting my kneecap that vibrates throughout my body first, the pain follows. I bite down hard on my lip to keep from screaming. Tears blur my vision, but I force them back. Weakness is not an option. Not here, not in front of them. I push myself to endure, to become someone else entirely. She is fearless, powerful, a creature of darkness. In this moment, I let go of who I am and embrace who I need to be. I take it all in, allowing the weakness to leave my body. The girl I see in the mirror is a stranger, a shell of the person I was when I arrived. This person only feels alive when pain courses through her veins. The energy surges through her veins. It's a twisted sort of euphoria, but it's all I have. All I need. I close my eyes, breathing out the fear, the weakness I cannot show here. My body stills, my nerves relax; I open my eyes; and I am her. I am the woman who can take whatever comes her way. I am a survivor. I can manage whatever is to come. Or so I thought.

Chapter Eight
Present

Upon returning home from Indiana, everything is eerily calm. We settle back into our day-to-day lives, getting lost in the mundane of it all. It's incredibly painful to look at my daughter. I want to cry just thinking about what I have brought into her life. She never asked for any of this. Now, there is a large probability that she's going to have her mother taken away from her. How am I going to survive leaving her if the time comes?

Every day, the weight of the load I am carrying seems to get heavier and heavier, and I am afraid that at any second I am going to break. It is almost worse that nothing is happening. I'm left imagining the worst possible scenario and imagining that happening.

I try to find comfort in the no-news-is-good-news philosophy. Isn't that what people always say? Though, I still have to play the part. I need to try and put a smile on my face, keep my guard up and be the person everybody thinks I am.

***

On September 2018, I finally find myself in my attorney's office, meeting for the first time. I have butterflies in my stomach the whole drive, not knowing what exactly I am walking into. I'm going to be hearing all the details of my charges, and the biggest piece of all, finally, hopefully, get the answer to if I am going to prison. And if so, for how long?

I pull up to his office, which is a renovated house turned into an office. I don't know why that is the first thing I notice, but I prepare myself to enter. I remember the circumstances in which he is appointed my attorney and hold onto the truth that it at least seems like there is something bigger working to put us together. My first impression is that he's casual not only in the way he dresses but also in how he presents himself.

We bond over hockey, which his son plays and so does my brother. The conversation flows effortlessly, and then playtime is over. He presents me with my folder which consists of every piece of documentation the Feds think they have on me and what they are seeking to charge me with. They are definitely embellished in the hopes of provoking fear to be used as a scare tactic for when they are ready to speak with me.

I sit there completely overwhelmed by the information; the number of details they have is astounding. So overwhelmed by the formality of it all, I will the floor to open underneath me and suck me in. It's an overwhelming amount of information. I understand that all of it is important, but at that moment, it isn't what I care about. What I need to know is what it all means regarding if I am going to prison or not. The honest answer is, it isn't black and white. It appears the answer is a lot like dealing with a lender at a bank. You are no longer a person; you have now become a number attached to other numbers that can be pled down or bought out. Up two, down one, three for this, five down for that. How much money do I have to buy my freedom? My problem, staring me straight into my soul, is that I unfortunately do not have the means to buy my way out of this. I'm at a poker game with no buy-in. I am out of the game before the first hand is ever dealt. That harsh truth leaves me at the mercy of the courts. My mind is spinning as the numbers dance and merge together to form a language I cannot understand. The end game, the fate of my future is held within the final number I am left with; I then take that number and open a big book that tells me in court currency what that number equals. My number, unfortunately, remains a question. The number of years I will spend in prison will go down or up depending on my level of cooperation and the amount of money I have to exchange. *How am I going to get enough money to buy my freedom?*

It's infuriating. Everything in life comes down to money. My stomach sinks, and I can't handle it any longer. All I end up getting out of the meeting is, yes, there is a definite possibility that I am going to prison. The only question that remains is for how long.

A month goes by and then another, and nothing is happening. It's quiet. There are no updates from my attorney, and even the government has gone quiet. It's like living two different lives—the life that I share with the public and my secret life. I get too comfortable in the quiet, take it for granted, thinking it means something it doesn't. I am naive to downplay it all, to even think for a moment that I am not worth the trouble. Surely, they have realized that I'm not that bad. I can twist and justify everything to convince myself that it is all going to quietly go away. But it doesn't.

***

It's now December 2018, and we are in the swing of the holidays, my favorite time of the year. My husband, daughter, and I are over at a friend's house, getting ready to have dinner when my phone alerts me that I have a text message. We are having fun, so I don't worry about checking it. I'll look at it later, but then another one comes, and then a few more after that within seconds of each other. That's all it takes for my curiosity to pique, so I go to look at my phone.

I have multiple messages but see there's one from my sister-in-law, so I open hers first. I want to make sure they are okay and that there isn't some sort of family emergency. As I open the message and read the first line, my heart feels like it crashes through the floor. I read the three words again, "You were indicted?"

I respond, my fingers moving as fast as I can make them move, feeling like every second counts and I need to know where she is getting this information from.

"What? I don't think so. Where did you see that?"

I hit send. I'm waiting; time is ticking; and I see the three dots. She's responding, but the dots stop, and there is still nothing.

Oh my gosh! I scream in my head. Panic threatens to escape from every part of my body. Again, three dots … Finally, the message. "You're on the news!"

I'm frozen; there is no air; there is nothing. Everything fades away, and all that is left is the dark hole I am emotionally spiraling down at this very moment. I look at my husband, and with the little air I can muster, I tell him, "We need to leave. Now."

As we get in the car, I am on high alert. I go to the news channels website, and there it is, an 82-page indictment, and my name is sitting pretty toward the top. Number 9. I go to their Facebook page, and there it is.

It's everywhere. The 5 o'clock news, the 6 o'clock news, the 10 o'clock news ... I'm sure you get it. My deepest darkest secret is out. Not only is it out, but it is a big neon sign that I am not going to be able to hide anymore.

I try calling my attorney, and of course, he doesn't answer. I then send him an email informing him that, apparently, I am indicted and a little head's up would have been nice. Now everyone is going to know. They are going to judge me, mock me, and throw me away. It's more than I can handle. I feel powerless. I have destroyed everything. I want to run. Run far away from everything and everyone. Luckily, we are already scheduled to leave in four days to fly and visit my family for Christmas. The timing couldn't have been better. It's my chance to say goodbye since I have no idea when I will be able to travel again or when I will even see them again. It has all hit the fan, and it is real, very real.

**

There is a dark cloud hanging over our heads as we make our journey to Indiana. The time spent with family is much needed and a blessing. I am informed while we are away that my indictment hearing is set for January 16, 2019. Three days after we are to arrive back home. My attorney also informs me that he is trying to wait until after the holidays to let me know about the indictment. He never expected it to be on the news. *Yeah, you and me both.*

I find it hard to enjoy anything that we do, trying to be present with my family, for my daughter, who has no idea what is going on. She's only three.

When we cheer and toast the new year, I can't help but cry. What do I have to look forward to? There is no optimism for the new year to come, no resolutions to be made. I know what the new year is going to bring me, and it isn't anything I am looking forward to. All I can think about is the loss, what I am going to have to face when I return, to go before a judge, in a room full of people that used to be my family a long time ago.

Chapter Nine
Past

"You can do this," Richard said to me, a pleading look in his eyes. We had been fighting more than usual at this point, usually about money and how he never thought we had enough of it. By this time, we had relocated to live closer to Julian and Andrea, propelling us into that life so much that it consumed most of our time. Richard was now depending on these "accidents" as our sole source of income. However, it seemed like it was never enough. We blurred the lines so far that we were no longer the people we were. I had become a shell of myself, having tossed aside my values and what I knew to be right from wrong. I put distance between my family and me and kept my friends at arm's length. My life had become a lie. When they asked what we did or where we got our money from or even what our uncle did, I always had to lie.

Don't get me wrong. There were good times. We traveled all over the world, taking cruises, and we spent a month traveling through Europe. When we were on vacation, we were our best selves. The stress of what was to come disappeared with each day, and we were able to just be us. No hiding, no secrets. It was always the heaviness of coming back home that made us lean further into ourselves, further into the circle where it felt safe. Every ounce of our lives, being completely controlled by our situation.

For me, it never got easier. I never felt okay with what we were doing, but that just made me the biggest hypocrite of them all. I didn't like the act but reaped from the reward. It was utter chaos. I now spent so much time in my character that after a while I stopped returning to who I was before and just allowed myself to fully become "her". Mentally, that's where I was the moment Richard came to me begging to do "this last one".

It was always just "this last one", but it never was. Here I stood, fighting every rational thought I had, pushing down the voice deep inside me that told me to walk away, but I couldn't. I couldn't leave my family. What would I be without them? Where would I go? I had nothing. I was so dependent on Richard for my survival, I had no choice.

Now, I know what you are thinking—you always have a choice. It's the consequences of those choices that most people don't want to deal with, and maybe in this situation, that was true, I could have chosen to get out, run as far away from this life as I could. The choice to do so would have been easy. To just go. The consequence of that "easy" choice, I would not have been able to bare. I loved him; I crazy loved him, which is why I stayed.

I had walked away from him once a few years into our relationship when I found out he had been unfaithful to me—a blow like nothing I had ever experienced. The betrayal I felt was gut-wrenching. How could he do this to me? We were perfect. We were the fairytale. Only, it turned out we weren't. I understood at that moment how a woman could harm someone who had hurt her so badly and not even realize it. Temporary insanity was a real thing, and I had experienced it that day. When I confronted him, I was filled with such rage, such sadness, and confusion, I only saw red. I had to run. I had to get away from him. I lasted twenty-four hours.

My phone rang in the middle of the night; it was his best friend on the other end of the phone telling me to give him another chance. Richard was devastated. He had attempted suicide by taking a bunch of pills and chased them with a bottle of Jack Daniels. I'm disappointed to say that's all it took. By the next afternoon, I was back home, kneeled in front of him, telling him it was going to be okay.

Allowing his excuses to be acceptable reasons for his actions and having such little self-respect for myself, I allowed him to convince me I was the problem. I found myself promising that I would do better. I would fix my mistakes so he wouldn't feel like I didn't need him anymore. I would make myself smaller so he could feel bigger. I would stroke his ego and be everything he needed. All the while leaving myself behind. Losing myself completely in the process, believing that if he didn't want me, if he didn't love me anymore then I had no value at all. Unfortunately, this wouldn't be the last time he would betray my trust or the last time he would manipulate me with threats of suicide. I allowed him to convince me that we needed this "one last time".

I opened the driver's side door of this vehicle that not a single part of me wanted to get into and positioned myself. I took a thousand deep breaths and waited. I knew what was supposed to happen, what we had discussed so many times before, but what ended up happening a few moments later was definitely not what we agreed to.

It was dark outside, and I was parked on a side street, waiting to be prepped, which is just a nice way of saying I was waiting to receive my injuries. It had been decided that the injury I was going to have for this "incident" would be a head injury that would result in a concussion along with a hurt shoulder. I had already begun to prep my shoulder before getting into the vehicle, pounding my shoulder by repeatedly using a glass Snapple bottle and absorbing the pain as it made contact over and over until I felt such a deep seeded bruise, I couldn't possibly imagine taking another hit. All my injuries were to be located on the left side of my body, as that would be the side of the vehicle that would take the impact. I closed my eyes as I sat there, taking deep breaths one at a time, trying my best to counter the pure panic and anxiety that was causing all the nerves in my body to revolt. "I'm fine," I said to myself. "It's going to be okay."

We talked about the injuries, and I expressed my hard limits, which sounds funny because for most people this whole process would be a hard limit. Setting limits on what I would and wouldn't accept for injuries or, more importantly, how I would receive those injuries was a way I felt like I was keeping a small amount of control in a situation, a world, where I felt completely out of control.

I saw Julian walking down the dark road toward me, dressed in all black. I almost didn't see him. He tapped on the window, and as I lowered it to see what he had to say, I immediately felt a jab to my head. I looked sideways and saw the glistening of metal from a razor blade. I was frozen from shock, trying to process what just happened when I was met with a blow to the very same spot, this time from a brick. I pulled away. The pain seared my brain, and all I saw was the blood that's flowing down my face.

"Here. Do it again," he said.

I didn't want to do it again. I was trying to protest, to get words to come out of my mouth when ... *crack!* Another whack. I looked at him, confusion in my eyes. This was not supposed to happen. This was my hard limit.

"No cuts," I said. "No cuts."

I heard him talking; it's all muffled as I tried to calm my body. My whole body was shaking and twitching. I must have been in shock. *Deep breaths.* There was so much blood. I couldn't do this. He wanted me to get in position, but my feet were twitching so much I can't even move them to get them on the pedal. *How am I going to get to where I need to be?* I had to calm down.

I cried out to Andrea and told her I couldn't do it. My body was shaking so much. I had no control over my movements.

She looked at me and said, "You can do this. Slow your breaths. Just breathe."

She slowly pushed my foot onto the gas pedal, supporting it with her own as we got into position. My breathing began to slow as I calmed down. *Head wounds bleed a lot. It's okay. You know this already*, I tell myself. *I'm ok. It's ok.* I repeated it over and over again until I started to believe my own lies.

I got into position and removed my foot from the gas pedal. I didn't know if I wanted to watch and see the other car coming or if I should just close my eyes and brace for the impact. I turned my head to the left, looking just quickly enough to see the lights of the oncoming car flash. It was the signal, so I knew it was time. There was no going back. No second thoughts. I pushed my whole body as far into the seat as I could, closed my eyes, let out a breath, and within what felt like seconds, we absorbed the crash, sending our car spinning in the opposite direction.

Dirt and debris flew all around us until we finally came to a stop some hundreds of feet away. It was quiet. Andrea and I looked at each other, silently confirming that we were both all right, and that now it was time for the real show to begin.

I slipped into character, slumping over in my seat, head leaning against the window as oncoming passers begun to arrive. The occupants of the other car started instructing them to call 911, and they did. I stayed in character, unconscious for just the right amount of time as the ambulance, firetrucks, and police all showed up. I began to come to, saying very little as I was loaded into the ambulance to be taken to the hospital. I spent six or seven hours in the hospital getting all the tests: x-rays, CT scan, and MRI, and then I was released and sent home.

Richard was happy; they all were. It was a perfectly executed job, well done by their standards. The only relief that I felt was that it was over. The rest of me felt empty and disgusted with myself, that I was so weak and angry with Richard for asking me to do it to begin with. I mourned for the young kids we used to be. Two kids in love, living in our cheap apartment, eating Ramen noodles and Oreos. Struggling to make ends meet but completely happy.

Chapter Ten
Present

January 16, 2019, arrives in what feels like a blink. We are back from our trip, back to the reality of our situation, prepping to go in front of the judge for the first time. I am all nerves, anxious that I must face not only the situation but all of them for the first time completely alone. With my husband having been named as a potential witness, he isn't allowed to be a part of any of my meetings or court appearances, which leaves me lost in my thoughts and fears for the long hour drive from my home to the courthouse.

I arrive early, which I always do, find a place to park, and walk up the large steps that lead to the front door of the building. Inside, I am greeted by officers and a metal detector. Once through the initial security, I find a seat in the corner and wait for my attorney to arrive. I place myself as far into the back as I can, knowing that it is very possible that I will also be seeing the others. Sure enough, after just a few minutes, Julian and Andrea arrive. They walk through the same security I do, but the only difference is their attorneys are there waiting for them. I ache for them to look in my direction, searching for that safety that they used to provide. It doesn't come.

Not only do they never look my way, but with a blink of an eye, they are gone, taken down a long hallway that I am sure will soon be my fate. I am getting antsy and frustrated that I am having to just sit here and wait for my attorney to show up. Is he late, or is everybody else early? The doors open again, a light breeze funneling in as I turn my head to see if my attorney is finally here, except it's not him. It is Richard arriving with his new wife who also, unfortunately, got tangled in his web just as I had those many years ago. I sink further back, hoping that he can't see me, and luckily, he doesn't seem to be paying attention to anything going on around him. I watch them, oddly fascinated as they converse with one another. This guy whom I had given so much of my life to was now a complete stranger to me.

He's aged, it seems, so much in the time we had been apart. The signs of constant stress and excessive drinking are written all over his face. I feel nothing. The anger for what he did to me, the constant betrayal, the lies—all of it is gone, and behind it, nothing remains.

My attorney enters at this time, and I stand up with as much confidence as I can muster and walk his way. After we exchange our pleasantries, we get on the same elevator as everyone who has gone before us and slowly climb to the fourth floor. The doors of the elevator open, and we are immediately ushered into the courtroom where we are all seated distant from each other.

I look around the room at all the people that had once been my family—the very comfort and security that I had once so deeply depended on—and realize how broken I truly was. There is no love in their eyes, no caring glances, no sign that they even know me at all. I am deep in these thoughts when I hear my name called, "Brittany Cecilia Jo." I looked up and realize it is my turn to go to the podium and enter my plea.

My attorney and I walk up, standing at the podium in front of the judge. The judge asks how I am going to plea, regarding my charges. I have already been instructed on what I am supposed to say, so I do what I am told and say, "Not guilty, your Honor." And that is it. One after another, they all go up, and one after another, they all say the same thing. Then it is over.

It's at this time that I am informed that I need to go down to the third floor and meet my newly appointed probation officer. *Oh great,* I think, *this seals the deal. I am officially in the system. I have a probation officer which means I am now on probation. Great!*

The doors of the elevator open, and to the right are the doors that lead into the probation office. All I have is a name, Mr. Banks. I walk up to the desk and sign in. I don't know what I expect a probation office to look like, but this is not it. It is an office filled with desks behind cubicles and three or four offices lining the back wall.

After waiting about ten minutes, a woman calls my name and tells me that Mr. Banks will see me now. I stand up and walk to the furthest office to the right of the building. I knock on the door and am pleasantly surprised by the face of the person on the other side of it. He doesn't look scary or mean as I had imagined; on the contrary, he has kind eyes and appears to be very nice.

Now, looking back, I can see that God had His hand in that specific probation officer getting assigned to me, but at that time, I am still not in a place to see that or even give it a thought. I am maybe half a toe in regarding God and how I feel about Him or don't feel about Him. At the time, I am unaware that God will make His presence known to me, and eventually, I will have to acknowledge Him, if I am ever going to be free.

My initial meeting with Mr. Banks is brief; he asks me some questions and starts what will end up being my ever-growing file. He gives me all the dos and don'ts of what I can and can't do now that I am in pre-trial. Pre-trial is the time you are on probation before you are found guilty or not guilty. The rules aren't too bad. Mostly, I am no longer allowed to travel outside of the state, and I have to check in with him upon his request. The thing I really like about him is even at our first meeting, he is so kind. He tells me he can tell that I am not a bad person. I am not someone he is going to have to worry about or think that there will ever be a chance that I'll find myself in this situation or his office again. I am just a good person that did a bad thing. That is true, right? Honestly, I don't know anymore.

Chapter Eleven
Past

After the "accident," Richard and I fell right back into our normal everyday lives. I think that was why it always felt so easy to compartmentalize what I did. It was one night, one part. I played a character, and then the very next morning woke up and got to be myself again. The two worlds did not coexist. There were a handful of people that knew both sides of me; everybody else only saw what I allowed them to see.

Richard began selling cars on the side to make more money and have a cover-up of some sort. At first, he would only leave town to pick up vehicles he had found online a couple of times a month, but as time went on, he was traveling more and more. Sometimes he would stay away for weeks at a time. It was when he was gone that I would realize just how lonely I was and how much I still depended on him for my happiness and my sense of security even after being together for all these years.

I started calling the few friends I had, begging them to come and stay with me. That worked for a while, but eventually, they stopped coming as they had their own lives to live. And, well, I really had no life at all.

Eventually, Richard put his friend in charge of me, and he began staying with me while he was gone. I had gotten a "real" job at this point, purely out of boredom and needing something to do with my time. It was his friend that would come to all my work events with me. We would go to the gym together and do anything I needed or wanted to do. He was the one that did it with me.

I used to think that, together, they made the perfect guy. I was so naïve, too blind to really see everything that was going on. I didn't notice how Richard and my relationship had become more business than it was love, how he was completely fine having someone else do life with me.

It was the night before he was about to leave on another one of his business trips. I could feel that his energy was off, but I just didn't know why. He was distant, not very affectionate. He wasn't looking at me the same. He kissed me differently than he had ever kissed me before, and lying in bed, the space between us could fill the sea. I felt it deep inside my gut that something wasn't right. I cried myself to sleep that night, knowing exactly what I would find when I could bring myself to look for it.

The next morning, I pretended to still be asleep when he came to say goodbye, knowing that if I looked at him, I wouldn't be able to hide the tears that would fall even though I would beg them not to. He kissed my forehead, and I knew he was already gone before he even left.

As I got ready for the day, all I could think about was getting the answers that I needed, and I knew exactly where I was going to look. I got to work and turned on my computer. Within minutes, I had our Verizon wireless bill up and saw everything I needed to see. There it was—call after call, text after text, all hours of the day and night, to one out-of-town number in particular. My eyes blazed; I couldn't believe I was here again, four years after I had caught him the first time. It's one thing to think that you know; it's another to know that you know. I didn't want to believe it. Maybe I was wrong; maybe it was work-related. I knew that wasn't the case, but I entertained the thought anyway. There was only one way to find out.

I picked up the phone, called the number, and waited while it rang. My heart pounded in my chest, and after about four or five rings, the voicemail recording came on and shattered any delusion I had that maybe I was wrong. It was a woman's voice on the other end with her young son giggling as they spoke in unison, letting you know they couldn't wait for you to leave a message and that they would call you back as soon as they could. That was the last dagger to my already broken heart. Not only was there another woman, but she also had a son.

I had wanted to have kids for the longest time, and he shut me down every time. I mean, I couldn't even get him to marry me, and we had been engaged now for ten years. I hung up the phone as quickly as I could. I knew everything I needed to know.

I went into the bathroom, secured myself in one of the stalls, and I sat on the floor, unable to contain my tears. This was it. I knew it was over. There would be no taking him back, no more letting his threats to harm himself stop me, no more believing his lies. He had broken me to the point of no return. Now, I just had to have the courage to face it.

As the day went on, it became increasingly obvious that they were either together at that very moment or at least had talked because, conveniently, for the first time in our eleven-year relationship, he didn't call me at work all day, not even once. It was such an obvious difference that even my boss at the time realized it and asked if everything was okay because he hadn't called.

Richard knew that I knew, and it was now a game to see who was going to break first and call the other. It was 5:30 pm that night when my phone finally rang; it was him. I answered the call and acted as nonchalantly as I could. He began the conversation just like it was any other day, asking me how I was, how work was. I shot one-word answers to him back-to-back, trying to force him into having to acknowledge that something was wrong. Finally, it came.

"Why didn't you call me when you got off?" he asked.

I responded with, "Because I know."

I heard the panic creep up into his throat as he started stammering his words.

"You know what?" I took a deep breath. The anger inside me is building higher and higher every moment that he acted like I was an idiot. "I don't want to talk about it right now."

He was full-on freaking out, pushing me and pushing me. I finally broke and gave into the hurt, the anger, the betrayal, all the emotions that were on the verge of exploding out of me. Everything I had done for him. Every sacrifice I had made. Every time I put his needs before mine. All the tears I had cried over him. It was all too much. I couldn't hold it in any longer.

I said the words like they were venom in my mouth. "I know that you are talking to her again. I know that you have been lying to me."

There was silence; he wasn't saying anything. I almost thought he hung up when I finally heard him take a deep breath and then began to frantically tell me how it wasn't what I thought, that I was wrong. It's not like that. Every lie that he had told before. Every word that I used to believe.

Finally, after I can't take any more of it, I finally say, "Richard, if you have ever loved me, please just tell me the truth. You have nothing to lose. It's over. The least you can do is tell me the truth. Is it the same girl from before?"

He told me that it was. That should have been enough. Why did I feel like I needed to know more? Why did it matter so much? Who cared about closure? Nothing was going to make me feel better, but I was apparently a glutton for punishment and thought it would be a great idea to follow up his response with my next question. "Did you ever stop talking to her?"

You know that saying, be careful what you ask for? I think that saying was created for this very moment. There was nothing in the world, in my wildest dreams, that could have ever prepared me for what he was about to say. The truth hurts, it was a dagger to your heart, and sometimes, we were better off without it.

"No. The first three years of our relationship it was just you and me."

I was, at this point, sick to my stomach, unable to wrap my mind around the fact the last seven years of our relationship had been a lie. I was so stupid. How did I not see it? Was it there all along, and I was too naive to see it? I was numb, no longer crying as there were no more tears left. I said nothing. All I left between us was the silence of me disconnecting the call.

Now, I will be honest with you. The few weeks that followed were horrible. They consisted of phone calls where we fought; phone calls where he begged me to forgive him; phone calls where he promised me everything under the sun. Now all of sudden he wanted to give me everything that he had refused to give me in the eleven years we had been together. I should have been mad. *How dare he?* After all this time, he only loves me the way I deserve to be loved when he is about to lose me. I wasn't sad, I was mad, really mad. Why wasn't I enough? Why has it always been so easy for people to toss me aside?

He showed up at the home we shared, fighting me every step of the way. It was his house too, and he wasn't going anywhere. He even moved into the basement just to make me uncomfortable and drive me crazy. He harassed me and made comments when I would leave the house. "Have fun with your boyfriend." A boyfriend that I didn't have.

He got so jealous when I would go somewhere and refused to tell him where I was going. On one incident, he kicked my bedroom door in that I had locked just to get away from him. Finally, I had enough. I couldn't live like this anymore, and I didn't have to. I called Julian, and he came over to mediate our separation and divide the assets we had accumulated as fairly as possible. I wasn't in a place where I could just walk away with nothing. It was the only way I was going to be able to get my own place and finally be free.

After a lot of back and forth, we finally agreed on everything, and Richard was told to stay away from the house until I moved out. I loaded up a U-Haul of the few things I had, got in my car, and drove away. I never looked back.

Chapter Twelve
Present

The timing of our return from our trip and my initial court date are days apart, which means we haven't had much time to face the backlash of everything now being out in the open. My indictment has run continuously on the news every hour for some time and is blasted on every local news channel's social media accounts. There is no way to not hear about it, which means our friends and family who have been kept in the dark from my secret life are now reading about my dirty laundry from the media perspective, and let's just say, it is one-sided.

It all falls apart quickly. Friends, who we thought were friends, no longer want anything to do with us. They have formed their opinions on the matter and decided that keeping their distance from us is the way to go. It's hard; we are already feeling isolated, alone, and ashamed. Now, our best friends of ten, twenty years are gone just like that, in a blink.

I stop leaving the house for fear of people seeing me, talking about me behind my back, judging me. I just want to hide. We spend more and more time at home, focusing on our family and trying to soak up every moment that we are being given, not knowing when the other shoe will drop and what new obstacle it will bring. We have made a New Year's Resolution to try and read the Bible in a year. It feels like such a cliché thing to do. Oh, your world is falling apart, turn to God, what else can you do? In truth, it is a cliché. We are not those people, and we don't go to church. We don't pray. We aren't Bible thumpers. I know it's a horrible term, but you know what I am talking about. It's the stereotype that every nonchurch goer gives to those people that do go to church, and you feel like they are pushing you to do the same. It's the pushing you that makes you feel judged, seen, exposed. We don't like that feeling, so we give them nicknames to make us feel better about not being them. I'm not even sure at this time in my life where God and I stand. Do I believe in Him? Does He believe in me? All are questions I am beginning to struggle with more and more each day as we finished chapter after chapter of God's word.

I am in the pit, the dark places in my mind where all my fears, anxiety, and failures are screaming at me, telling me I am nothing, undeserving, unloved, that I ruined everything. They scream that I am never going to be forgiven, that I destroyed my family and didn't deserve to be a mother. I have become everything I never wanted to be.

We decide to read the Bible in chronological order, and while we are reading Job, I am hit with the first scripture that touches me deep inside. This is the first time a "truth bomb" as I like to call them is released and begins breaking down all of the lies, I have been carrying for so long.

Job 11:13-19 says, "Yet if you devote your heart to him and stretch out your hands to him, if you put away the sin that is in your hand and allow no evil to dwell in your tent, then you will lift up your face without shame; you will stand firm and without fear. You will surely forget your trouble, recalling it only as waters gone by. Life will be brighter than noonday, and darkness will become like morning. You will be secure, because there is hope; you will look about you and take your rest in safety. You will lie down, with no one to make you afraid, and many will court your favor."

It is like the scripture was written just for me. Like God is saying, "Hey, I see you." I want to feel that way, to live without shame for who I am and what I do, to no longer be paralyzed by my fear, to find hope instead of dread. I feel a little piece of me crack, and I am not sure what scares me more, staying where I am—I have become comfortable in these feelings after all—or going through the pain and heartache of getting to the other side once and for all. I don't know, but I know through this journey I am going to find out.

It's as if that crack opens a tiny link between me and God, and He is determined to keep pushing, keep fighting to get to me because it isn't long after that one of our neighbors randomly knocks on our door.

Now, this neighbor, she is a church person. Ya know, the type of people we discussed earlier. She leaves pamphlets on our windshields and notes in our mailbox; it appears she really wants us to go to church. Obviously, I threw them all away. I certainly don't have the time or energy for that. Well anyway, we let her in. I am on edge about why she is here. She is very nice and always seems genuine, the kind of person you want to be friends with, not the kind of friends I have.

After we make small talk for a while and she spends some time with my daughter who loves when she gets to see her, her intention for coming over is finally revealed. She wants to invite us to church that Sunday. There it is. I immediately become uncomfortable. I don't want to tell her no, but I don't want to lie to her either. I am definitely not going to church. I am in the baby step stage, not the throw myself into the fire stage.

She explains how it was Mother's Day weekend, and she thinks it would be the perfect opportunity for us to try the church out. It sounds horrible, so I decline the nicest way I can. "Oh, no thank you." I have no desire to go to church, and I certainly don't want to walk into a building full of people who don't know me and will judge me on the worst things I have ever done. I am on the news for goodness' sake and in the local smalltown paper. I basically have a neon sign over my head that says, "Hey, it's me. I'm the criminal that everyone is talking about whether what they're saying is true or not, it doesn't matter."

I am ready to thank her for coming when to my utter shock my husband says he thinks it might be nice and we should go. Nice? There is nothing that's going to be nice about that. Great, now it's two versus one. I just want the conversation to end so I reluctantly agree that I guess we can go to church on Sunday. Clearly satisfied with the outcome, our lovely neighbor says goodbye, and as I slowly close the door behind her, I shoot my glance at my husband and say, "Really?" but he just smiles, walks over to me, gives me a hug, and says, "Don't worry. It will be fine." Dang it! I am going to church.

***

Sunday morning comes, and as a family, we get ready for church. I'm anxious all morning. I give myself pep talks, trying to convince myself that I can do it. It really will be fine. Though, it isn't working. I am fighting every natural reaction my body is having. I am a runner. I run from problems, conflict, and basically anything that challenges me. It's how I was raised, and I have been running ever since. It appears, however, that I won't be running from this.

We load into the car and begin our very quick trip to the church. We pull into the parking lot, and there is a pit in my stomach. I'm having trouble relaxing, and I'm losing my nerve with every second. I feel like I am on the verge of a panic attack. I'm freaking out. I have so much guilt and shame inside my body that I can't even get it together long enough to walk into a church.

I look at my husband and tell him I can't go. I've changed my mind; we can try again another time. Bless his heart, he just smiles at me, tells me everything will be fine, and gets out of the car. *Oh no, this is happening. Ok, legs, I need you to move.*

I open my car door and inch out ever so slowly. I take a deep breath and walk over to where my husband is waiting for me with our daughter, grab his hand as if my life depends on it, saying with each step we take, getting closer and closer to the door, "I don't want to do this. I don't want to do this," but we are doing it.

We open the doors, and when we walk through them, I am not prepared for what comes next. It feels like I am having an out-of-body experience—thank you, anxiety—and I am in a scene from a movie. The sunlight shines through just perfectly, lighting our path, as everyone standing in the hall sees us for the first time and begins to come over, one after another after another. They know exactly who we are upon hearing our names, but they tell us how happy they are that we decided to come. They don't condone me for my crimes. It all feels so strange and wonderful at the same time.

During that first church service, I am an emotional wreck. I have never felt rawer and more exposed than I did in that hour and fifteen minutes. It's like every song they are singing is directed at me. Every word the pastor speaks is a straight connection to my heart. The tears are flowing uncontrollably. I am a mess. I don't understand what is happening, but I know something inside me is changing.

As we drive home, I am unable to find any words to express my thoughts. I sit in silence, trying to process the experience we have just had, the feelings that are overwhelmingly inside me. I'm not sure if I like feeling so vulnerable. I'm exposed. Everyone can see my deepest darkest fears, the shame I am carrying, the utter despair and sadness with every teardrop that falls from my eyes. It seems so overwhelming. I'm not sure if I can go back there. Did I even want to? Maybe it's safer just reading our Bible at home for now.

Chapter Thirteen
Past

As I drove away, leaving Richard behind, I couldn't believe I had actually done it. For so long, I thought I would be stuck in that cycle, forever taking him back. But now, here I was, Brittany without Richard.

It was strange to think about, but I realized I wasn't in love with him anymore. When did that happen? Was it a gradual process, a slow chipping away at my heart with every heartbreak, tear, and fight? Or was it sudden, the final blow that shattered my heart beyond repair? I didn't know, but I was finally free to find out who I really was. For the first time in my life, I had the chance to figure out who I was without anyone else's expectations weighing me down. Who was I? What did I like? What did I want? I had spent so long trying to please others that I had forgotten what made me happy. But now, I was excited to discover the real me.

Amid this self-discovery, I decided it was also the perfect opportunity to work on mending the relationship with my mother. We started speaking again when I called her the following August after I'd run away for her birthday. I had already turned eighteen and used her birthday as an excuse to reconnect. We kept our conversations light, making an unspoken agreement not to discuss the past or any details regarding my running away. It was a superficial relationship, but at least we were talking again. As a girl, I've always craved a relationship with my mother, no matter the circumstances.

After all those years of superficial conversations and distance between us while I was with Richard, I was grateful that now that I was starting my life over, I could finally talk to her without having to hide aspects of my life anymore. I ached to be close to her and to finally have the relationship with her I always dreamed of. I knew that the road to healing our relationship would be long and winding, but I was willing to take it one step at a time. I looked to the future, and I felt hopeful of what was to come, that one day my mother and I would be close and there would no longer be any bridges between us.

I also wanted to work on my relationships with my friends. I was lucky to have some amazing friends who had been there for me through thick and thin. They supported me every step of the way, even when I didn't deserve it. I was grateful for their love and support, and I knew that I had to do better by them.

Shortly after my breakup a mutual friend reached out and told me he was going through a divorce. I was surprised when I heard the news and, at the request of one of my friends, decided to invite him to come hang out with us. We had always hit it off, had a lot of fun together, and could make each other laugh. We were both going through a period of change and transition, and it was comforting to have each other to lean on.

Over time, he went from being a casual friend to being one of my closest companions. We talked on the phone every day, sharing our fears, our failures, and our dreams for the future. I confided in him about my therapy appointments, and he spoke to me about his children, expressing how much he loved them and how afraid he was of hurting them. We laughed; we cried; and we talked about everything under the sun.

As time went on, I couldn't imagine my life without him in it. It felt amazing to finally have someone I was able to be my raw, true self with; there was no need to impress him or put on a façade. It was just so easy to be around him. One day, he surprised me by suggesting that we should kiss.

"Why?" I asked him.

He replied with a laugh, "To see if we like it. Are we just best friends, or could we be something more?"

I wasn't sure what to think. Yes, I had always thought he was attractive, and to be honest, my feelings were growing by the day, but I didn't want to ruin our friendship. I told him my fears, that I didn't want to lose him. He assured me that we could always go back to being just friends if the kiss didn't work out. I agreed to think about it, and we dropped the subject for the time being.

A few days later, he picked me up on my lunch break, and we went to the park to walk around. I was nervous because we hadn't addressed the kissing situation yet, and I knew it was going to come up.

Once it was in the universe, it was all I could think about. I started picturing what it would be like to kiss him, to be close to someone who knew me so well. His piercing blue eyes blazing straight into my soul, unable to hide anything from him. I was a ball of nerves. I was positive about what my decision was, but it all became clear when we got out of the truck and his hand found mine. It fit perfectly, and I felt unequivocally safe. I couldn't help the smile that crossed my lips as we walked. I was just about to open my mouth to speak when a stranger walked by us and told us what a cute couple we were. It was the strangest thing to have happen, completely out of nowhere, but it confirmed everything that I already knew. I was going to kiss this guy.

I squeezed his hand and said, "Okay."

"Okay, what?"

"Okay, I'll kiss you."

I glanced up and saw the smile on his face, and I couldn't help but smile too. Butterflies began to dance in my stomach as I anticipated the act. *What would it be like? Was I making a mistake?* We came upon a beautiful ginormous willow tree on the side of the pond we were walking around that had a bench a few feet from it. He headed in that direction. *This is it; it's going to happen. Oh gosh. Is he going to be a good kisser? Am I?* I was lost in my thoughts as we sat on the bench. I could see he was thinking, abnormally quiet, and just when I couldn't take the weirdness anymore, he got up from the bench took my hand, and led me to the tree.

"What are we doing?"

"Just come here," he said.

He led me to the tree and pressed my back up against the trunk. I looked up at him, straight into those piercing blue eyes that I had now thought of more times than I cared to admit, and I knew this was it. This was the moment we were going to kiss. Of course, he would try and make it special. Of course, he would treat it like it was the most important thing to him. He leaned his head down, and I swear I stopped breathing just before our lips touched. Then, that was all there was, him and me and this kiss. Everything else faded away. It was soft and hungry at the same time. Our lips danced together perfectly. The heat rose in my stomach, aching to explode out of me. It went on forever and not long enough. As our lips parted and we stared into each other's eyes, I didn't know what to say. I didn't know how to explain how I was feeling or even if I should. What if he didn't feel the same way? What if the best kiss of my life was just an okay kiss for him? Doubt began to plague me when he smiled at me and casually said, "Yeah, we aren't friends."

I couldn't help but laugh. It was the perfect thing to say to sum up everything I was feeling as well. Now, I wanted to kiss him all the time. Our relationship took off on that day.

We were now spending most of our free time together. Tuesday nights became my favorite. He would come over to the apartment I shared with my best friend, and the three of us would go to Zumba class and then come home and watch Vampire Diaries. He was the complete opposite of anything I knew.

He taught me to ride four-wheelers and made me more adventurous. We had bonfires and spent time in nature. We were always laughing and had the best time together. I finally had someone to dance with me. I won't say that it was always perfect. Two broken people coming together, whether you wanted to be or not, were still broken. We were madly in love, and we showed up every day for each other, wanting to be the best version of ourselves that we could be.

It was a few months later, on Christmas morning, that I found myself at that very same park, under that very same willow tree covered in snow, with that very same perfect man on his knee asking me to be his wife. It was magical, perfect, and I couldn't have been happier.

A few months later, I found out that I was pregnant. I had always wanted to be a mother. Other girls dreamed of being a doctor, a marine biologist, a singer, a dancer, but I ached to be a mother. I wanted that relationship, someone to love unconditionally and that would love me back. I wanted to do it right. I was going to right every wrong that I had experienced. It was an answered prayer, and then, it was gone.

***

I woke up the morning of our combined bachelor/bachelorette weekend camping trip blissfully excited and ready to celebrate with our closest friends. I went into the bathroom, and there wasn't anything in the world that could prepare me for that moment when I saw blood on the toilet paper where there wasn't supposed to be any. My heart sank into the pit of my stomach, and my gut told me something was wrong. I just knew. I called my mother and told her what was happening. She remained calm, told me that sometimes bleeding was normal. I needed to stay positive and try to relax this weekend. If I got myself worked up, it wouldn't help the situation. She asked me if there was a lot of blood or a little. At the time, it was just a little. Still hesitant but more optimistic, we headed out for our weekend celebrations, and I did my absolute best to remain positive. I just needed to stay calm, I told myself. It was going to be okay; it had to be.

We arrived at our destination and began enjoying ourselves with our friends. A couple hours after our arrival, the cramping started. It was light at first, so, again, I tried to ignore it and stay focused and positive. We went to sleep later that night, and I couldn't shake the feeling that something was wrong. I wanted to be that person; the person that could remain positive. The person that positive things happened to. It just never seemed like that was my fate.

The next morning, I woke up, the cramping had intensified, and my lower half was covered in blood. Any hope, any optimism, any chance that I wasn't losing this baby left as quickly as my sweet angel had appeared. We knew what was happening, and I needed to get to the hospital.

The hospital was two hours away from where we were camping. The drive was agonizing. I couldn't stop crying. I was utterly and completely devastated. We arrived at the hospital, and I was taken straight back. I put on the gown and sat on the cold table. They rolled in an ultrasound machine and set me up. They searched, moved it all around for minutes that seemed like hours, and then that was it. I saw it in their eyes. When they looked at me, the expression on their faces … there was nothing. My baby is gone.

"I'm sorry. There is no heartbeat."

The crushing words broke me into a million pieces. I stared at the screen, willing for the emptiness to be filled. Thinking if I just stared at it long enough, I would find something. I had to, but nothing ever came. I slowly got dressed and was given some pills to help with the pain. The doctor instructed me to go home and get some rest. It would take a few days for me to pass the fetus, but I could do it at home. It all felt so unpersonal, so matter of fact.

We left the hospital, and I felt empty. The despair of the loss was too much to carry. I didn't know how I could possibly have any more tears to cry. I was wrong.

They don't warn you how painful the process is going to be. How much blood is going to leave your body, how scary it is going to seem, how it crushes you deep down in your soul every time you have to sit on the toilet in excruciating pain while you leave piece after piece of your hopes and dreams behind. It is a loss that never leaves you no matter how much time passes.

As it is with life, time moved on; we moved forward; and every day, it got a little easier. We leaned into each other and stayed focused on the good things in our life.

We were married in August 2014, in the most beautiful wedding of my dreams. We were surrounded by love, and it was the perfect day. We honeymooned in Kauai, Hawaii, falling in love with everything about that magical place. The slowness of the pace. The peace the ocean brought our souls. I was completely happy and found it hard to go back home.

A few weeks after returning home from our honeymoon, we relocated to Indiana. I had made the decision that I wanted to go home after my awful breakup and wanted a fresh start. My husband unselfishly agreed to let me try and do just that. I wanted to be by my family, to try and heal the wounds of the past.

It was shortly after we arrived in Indiana that I learned I was pregnant again. If I am being honest, yes, of course, I was thrilled, completely happy to have another opportunity to be a mother. I was also terrified. I couldn't stop worrying that I was going to lose this one too.

The doctors took every precaution to make sure the baby was fine. They checked my levels weekly, in the beginning, making sure they doubled and were growing like they were supposed to. I was classified as a high-risk pregnancy, and that made me even more anxious.

Every month that went by, my worries eased a little bit. I had horrible morning sickness. They would say that's good; that meant the baby was growing.

Then six months in, my worst fears, the worst event in my life seemed to be happening again. Blood. I went to the bathroom, and there was blood. This couldn't be happening. Why was I being punished? Had I done so much bad in my life that God was going to keep punishing me? Was I destined to always suffer?

I happened to be with my mom that day, so as soon as I came out of the bathroom, I told her what was happening. She brought me to the hospital that she worked at, and I was admitted immediately. We called my husband, and they began hooking me up to all these machines, monitoring me and the sweet little girl that was growing inside me. I tried to remain calm. My blood pressure was very high. I needed to breathe, to relax. The doctor came in, and I swear to you there wasn't a single part of me that was ready for what he said.

"You're in labor."

My head spun. Panic threatened to escape every cell of my body. I couldn't be in labor. It was too early. My mind drifted away, going to the dark place where my fears were. One after one. Hitting me with everything they had. I wasn't listening to what the doctor was saying. I wasn't even in my body anymore. Then, things started happening around me. I tried to focus. What were they doing? What was the plan? I fought with every ounce of strength that I had to face the moment, to be present. I had to protect my baby. I calmed down and came back to reality.

The doctor was speaking to me, his sounds finally forming words. "We are going to try and stop your labor," he said. "I am going to put this medication in your IV, and then we are just going to have to wait and see."

I waited, and, thankfully, my labor stopped. I was stable enough to be sent home, and I was put on bed rest for a few weeks to ensure everything stayed the way it was supposed to. Bed rest was torture, but I would do anything for this baby, anything I had to do to keep her safe.

Things calmed down and went back to normal after bed rest, and I tried my best to find joy in the pregnancy. It was supposed to be a happy joyful time. I felt that way sometimes, but truthfully, I spent most of the time in agonizing fear that at any moment something was going to go wrong again. I was reaching the end of my pregnancy, and my blood pressure was continuing to grow higher and higher. I was swollen and unwell. It was determined by my doctor that I would be put back on bed rest, my blood pressure monitored multiple times a day until I hit thirty-seven weeks, and then I was going to be induced.

Induction day came, and I couldn't be happier to finally give birth to her. I no longer had to carry the burden of worrying about her inside me, of not being able to keep her safe. I truly believed that once she was born, everything would be better.

On June 3, 2015, after eighteen hours of labor, I finally met her. She was finally in my arms, and the sense of relief that I felt was all-encompassing. I had her. She was safe, and she was ours.

Chapter Fourteen
Present

In March of 2019, my final plea deal offer arrives from my attorney. These are the terms and charges I am supposed to agree to, and these will be the charges I am pleading guilty to. The short version is, I am to plea guilty to four counts. The charges are for mail fraud, conspiracy to commit mail and wire fraud, and conspiracy to commit health care fraud. Class C felonies that hold a potential maximum imprisonment sentence of up to twenty years for the mail and wire fraud charge, the conspiracy to commit health care fraud holds a maximum sentence of up to ten years imprisonment, the court having the authority to impose consecutive sentences for each conviction.

Also, upon release from prison, I am facing three years of supervised release, restitution, and a fine not to exceed $250,000.00. Reality is rearing its ugly head and is determined not to grant me any opportunity to stick my head in the sand. Things are getting real, and they are getting real, quickly. The air begins draining from my lungs, the heaviness of what I am facing sinking me further into the quicksand of my life, and it seems with every movement I make, I sink a little deeper. I see no way out. This is the only opportunity they are giving me to avoid trial, a trial in which I am certain a jury of my peers will fine me on the higher end of the maximum sentence allowed.

I read the plea agreement to my husband, the crushing weight of the silence hanging in the air between us. What could either one of us say? He knows there are no words of comfort he can give me, no false hopes that things are going to work out okay. I see no light ahead, no hope to be found, and I know there isn't anything I can say to him to bring him any comfort as the words on the pages are like a neon sign blazing red that he is, in fact, going to be losing his wife, for how long we don't know, and my daughter is going to be without her mother.

The darkness starts to take over all the space inside me it can find, eating up any hope it can devour like a parasite with an insatiable appetite.

The hopelessness I feel is so consuming, I am getting scared, no longer just of the impossible situation I currently find myself in but of the darkness growing inside of me. I know the darkness well. I know how easily it is to concede to its will. I have felt its grip before and barely come out with my life. I often think about a quote from *Twilight* that Bella says. Now, I know, I'm talking to you about *Twilight*, but bear with me. In the movie, Bella states, "Death is peaceful, easy. Life is harder."

When I heard those words when I was younger, I felt them deep in my soul. I know the pain, the ache, the very thought that giving up will be so much easier than continuing to live, which seems to be one of the hardest things to do. I feel myself going back to that quote now, and to be honest, I don't know if I have any fight left in me. Satan has his grip so tight on me that even as I search for it, long for it, I can't find a way to make any of it okay. I have to make a choice. Am I going to concede to the darkness, give in, and let it take me away? Or am I going to fight? Fight for my life, fight for my future, my husband, and my sweet daughter.

I find the word *abject*, the official definition being, to be utterly wretched or hopeless. Miserable, forlorn; dejected. Utterly wretched seems about right. I stall out as long as I can, but eventually, I have to sign the deal. It only takes three seconds to seal my fate. Three seconds to end my whole world as I know it. The worst part is, it's my fault. I have done this to myself and to my family. The guilt and shame I carry become an anchor to my soul.

Chapter Fifteen
Present

The first year of my daughter's life brought a lot of challenges along with a lot of joy. I found myself struggling with depression after she was born. Exhausted from lack of sleep, unable to soothe her as she cried every night, every two hours. (Little did I know, she would do this until she turned one.) Breastfeeding was a challenge; she wouldn't latch. Everything was adding up, and the conclusion was I was a horrible mother. I felt sad and unable to cope, and at my lowest point, it kills me to admit, I left. I left her and my husband, got in my car, and just drove away. I didn't know where I was going or what I was going to do. I just felt so out of control that I ran. I told you, that's what I do.

Anyway, I called my friend, pouring out my heart and soul to her. Every shortcoming I felt, every way that I did not feel good enough. I talked and talked and talked. It wasn't until I had unloaded everything I had and began to calm down that I realized where I was. I had driven to a church and was currently sitting in their parking lot.

The irony of that wasn't isn't lost on me, but still, I don't acknowledge that it is another time in my life that God uses to try and reach me. Nope. Not me. I'm sitting over here like Little Richard—you can keep on knocking but you can't come in.

The phone call ended with my friend encouraging me to go home and helped me to realize that it wasn't that I was a horrible mother, I was exhausted, and I needed to ask for help.

Slowly, as I was honest about my struggles, I got some rest, and with rest and some help with baby shifts, things got easier. We began to fall into a groove. Unfortunately, while things were starting to fall into place in our home, things were not going so well in Indiana. We missed the mountains and the beauty of where we lived before. The relationships I so desperately wanted to mend were no better off, and I often found myself being constantly let down and disappointed in the fact they weren't progressing in the ways I had hoped.

After a lot of late-night conversations between my husband and me, we decided the right thing for our family was to move back home where we felt in our hearts we belonged.

So, when my daughter was eight months old, we traveled across the country, back to where it all began. We bought some property and decided we were going to build our dream home on it. After all, my husband was a contractor. It was going to be an amazing journey, and we were going to live in a travel trailer together on the property while we did it.

It felt good to be back. We were back with our friends, and the mountains greeted us with their pure beauty. Returning home also meant I was back with Julian and Andrea. They met my daughter and became just as in love with her as everyone else did. We started getting together again for dinners, met up for boat rides, and even took a trip together. It was amazing how being around them was always such a comfort to me, and I was so grateful that they accepted my husband in their lives when they didn't have to.

They were my family; even after everything happened with Richard, they didn't give me up. A piece of me that had been missing was put back into place, but it didn't take very long for the phone call that I knew would come to come. I knew it would at some point. I just hoped I was wrong.

It was Julian, and he wanted to meet up to discuss a favor he needed from me. He was in a bind and knew he could count on me to help him out. My mind was already aware of the direction this conversation was going to go without even having to ask what it was about. I could feel it deep inside to the very core of my stomach. My insides trembled as the same feeling of panic I had spent such a large part of my life accustomed to crashed through me like a train rolling off its tracks. I had already told him that wasn't my life anymore. I had moved on from those things. I have a daughter now. I was different. I needed to be different. He claimed this was another "last one."

He pulled at my weakness when he said, "I want you to have the amazing life you and your family deserve; you have been through so much. This could help you be do that."

That was it; he got to me. I fell for it. We met for dinner, and I found myself transcending back in time to my old life, the old girl I used to be. At least I thought I wasn't her anymore, but the fact that I was even considering this conversation proved that I was still, without a doubt, her. I was still weak, still seeking my value and self-worth in what others thought of me. I was still broken.

To be broken means to have been fractured or damaged, no longer in one piece or working order. I was unquestionably broken. I found myself agreeing to one more time, one more "job". I could never say no to him. I knew it, and he knew it too. I made him promise me this would be it, that he would never ask me to do this again. He agreed and said he wanted nothing more than to see my family and me happy and living our dreams. I believed him, but maybe I shouldn't have.

A few months later, I found myself on an airplane, headed to fulfill the commitment I had so tragically agreed to do. I arrived the day before which gave me time to unwind, if that was possible, meet the other "players", and go over plan details.

When I say it was a well-oiled machine, it was. Every detail to the minute was planned and thought out. I knew the speech, details, and my job like the back of my hand. I tried to sleep, knowing tomorrow was going to be a very long day.

Sleep, as I assumed, did not come. I was plagued with fear, anxiety, stress, and worry. Now on top of all that, disgust and shame coursed through me for even being there in the first place. Maybe it was good that I wasn't okay; maybe it meant that somewhere deep down inside of me there was a part that wasn't dead. Maybe it was that small part that would one day save me.

Morning came, as it always does; the final plans were set; and now, I had to wait. The wait was agonizing. Too much time to think, ponder, and second guess every decision you have ever made. Self-reflection is hard, and that was a journey I was not ready to embark on at this moment.

Finally, it was time to go. I took one last look in the mirror, closed my eyes, took a deep breath, and when I opened them, I was once again "her". I looked at her in the mirror. "Hello, old friend." Her eyes were dark, cold, and distant. There was no emotion, no sense of feeling at all. The trials I had endured formed her in the darkest parts of me. Each one was a piece of stone used to create the wall that she used as her armor. It was her armor that made it possible for her to get into that car, be the good soldier, take the blows, absorb the impact, and play the part. It was easy for her. She didn't have to face the consequences of her choices, and she didn't have to hate herself for the things she did. No, I was the one left to carry the weight of it all, and I had no one to blame but myself.

When I got into the car, I was numb. Sometimes it scared me how easily I could become her. How easy it was for "her" to take over. The allure of the dark side was as tempting as a black hole, pulling you in with a force so strong that you risk losing yourself in its depths and becoming one with the shadows. I completed the task, did everything I was supposed to do, and when I returned to the hotel room, I cried. It was getting harder to get back to myself. The darkness threatened to consume me, to drag me down into its depths and snuff out my light. I had to fight. I refused to surrender, and with every ounce of strength I possessed, I pushed back against the shadows and found my way back to the light, to who I truly was, and I vowed that this time really would be my last time. I was petrified that if it wasn't, I might lose myself all together.

The plane ride home was a somber one. I kept thinking about my daughter and how I had let her down, my husband who didn't want me to go, but I did anyway. The guilt of my weakness was almost too much to bear. I had chosen my old life over my new one, and I didn't know it yet, but there was going to be hell to pay.

***

Signing my plea deal, actually pleading guilty for the things I have done, changes everything. No longer do I have the luxury of pretending this is all a nightmare; no longer am I able to convince myself that this all isn't happening. No. Now I must experience the pain of the reality of my situation; I need to accept the fact that I am going to prison and there is nothing I can do about it. The unanswered question that remains is for how long and where? Will I be close by? Will I get to see my family? Will I want my daughter to even see me that way? It is unbearable. I have reached rock bottom.

Learning how to exist in my life is becoming more and more challenging by the day. I am in this purgatory of waiting—waiting to hear from my attorney, waiting to hear from the government, waiting to receive my sentencing date, waiting, waiting, waiting. I don't know how to live a normal life when my life is the furthest thing from normal.

It is in the midst of my waiting that my attorney reaches out and says the government had requested a meeting with me for the next day. I try to remain calm, try not to think too much of it, but I just can't figure out what they need to discuss with me. I signed the papers and agreed to everything they asked. What else can I possibly give them?

I drive to the courthouse the next morning and am quivering with anticipation, but not in a good way. I have no idea what I am getting myself into. I arrive at the district attorney's office where my attorney is waiting for me. We exchange pleasantries and then I ask him if he knows what this is all about. He says he doesn't have very many details. He only knows that they want to talk to me about one of the other individuals in my case who ran. He thinks it's Julian's son. That surprises me as I haven't talked to his son in years and have no idea what information I can possibly give them. Unfortunately, once we are finally escorted back to the office for our meeting, I learn the shocking truth.

When I entered the room, the district attorney is there along with the Marshall and a woman who doesn't bother introducing herself. They begin talking, and as they are talking, my heart pounds in my chest as I try to comprehend what I am hearing. The world around me seems to fade away as I float in disbelief.

The silence wis deafening, and the darkness is all-encompassing as I struggle to hold myself together. It feels as if I am in a nightmare, a place where nothing makes sense, and everything is turned upside down. Every fiber of my being is in shock, and I can't shake the feeling that I am about to wake up any moment. But as the truth sinks in, I realize that this *is* real. The things they are saying shatter my heart like glass into a million pieces so small it would be a miracle if it can ever be put back together. Julian has run, and they want me to tell them where he is. I have no idea. I never in my life thought he could do that, abandon us when he gave his word that he would always be there, that he would take the punishment. He broke his promise. He has abandoned me, and I can't speak.

I tell them I don't know, don't have any idea where he might be. I think they realize that I truly have no idea by the shock I am currently sitting in, and they tell me I can go home but to call them if anything comes to mind or if he reaches out to me. For some reason, they think he cares about me enough to reach out, but I now know that isn't true at all.

As I exit the office, I feel like I am in a daze, completely lost in my thoughts. The world around me seems to fade away as I struggle to process what has just happened. I don't even remember how I made it to my car; everything is a blur. My mind is consumed with the shocking news that has been revealed to me, and I can't shake the feeling of disbelief and confusion. As I sit in my car, my thoughts continue to spiral, leaving me feeling more lost than ever before.

As I pulled out of the parking lot, tears stream down my face, blurring my vision of the road ahead. The radio is on, but I can't hear the music over the sound of my own sobs. The weight of his betrayal sits heavily on my chest. It's as if I am in a bubble, cut off from the rest of the world. My mind is spinning with questions and doubts, and I can't shake the feeling that everything I think I knew, everything I believe down to my very core is a lie.

The drive home feels endless, as if time has slowed down to torture me further. All I can do is let the tears flow and allow the pain to consume me until there is nothing left.

When I arrive home, I recount the meeting to my husband, and the words feel like knives as I speak them. He's immediately filled with anger about the situation. I long to feel the fiery burn of anger instead of the hollow numbness that consumes me, a reflection of the profound sense of betrayal and emptiness I feel in the pit of my stomach. But for now, I am held captive by my unwavering loyalty and love for him, hoping that one day, I will be able to unleash the full extent of my emotions, including the seething rage that lays just beneath the surface.

I can't focus on the hurt I am feeling. I need to make a conscious effort to move forward and focus on my family. We are facing an impossible situation, and I know that giving outside situations any more of my energy will only make things worse. They need me, and they are where my loyalty needs to belong.

So, we slowly begin to fall back into our routine, grasping onto any sense of normalcy we can find in a world where nothing seems normal. It's a small comfort, but it's something to hold onto as we navigate these uncertain times.

We get more consistent in reading the Bible every morning. My husband continues to go to work every day while I stay home with our daughter, absorbing every precious second that I have with her, and we begin going to church every Sunday. To the outside world, we look like a normal family. If only that's true.

It's during one of our morning Bible readings when something begins to shift in me. We are reading the book of John, and when we get to John 8:7 which reads, *When they kept on questioning him, he straightened up and said to them, "Let any one of you who is without sin be the first to throw a stone at her,"* I feel it through my bones. I have been tossed aside, mocked, judged, and hated by people I know will never be able to stand there and throw their own stones. They are sinners just like me; the only difference is the worst thing they have ever done wasn't broadcast to the world on the news, and they don't have to worry about their secrets being exposed in the paper. Their secrets stay hidden.

The more I read, the more I feel Jesus calling me to Him. Matthew 11:28 says, *"Come to me, all you who are weary and burdened, and I will give you rest."* It keeps going. Psalm 34:17-20 says, *When the righteous cry for help, the Lord hears and delivers them out of all their troubles. The Lord is near to the brokenhearted and saves the crushed in spirit. Many are the afflictions of the righteous, but the Lord delivers him out of them all. He keeps all his bones; not one of them is broken.*

With each scripture we read, I can feel the walls of my shame, anguish, fear, hopelessness, all the weight I have been carrying cracking, piece by piece.

I won't lie to you and tell you I miraculously felt better and that everything went away. That is not this story. I will tell you that it was a start. There was a small spot deep down inside me that began to flicker with light, hoping that one day things would be okay again. One day, I would become the person I always hoped to be but wasn't. That there was a purpose in all of this. It was that small light that I focused on.

I begin to no longer hide when we go to church. I sing worship songs, tears streaming down my face like a dam that has burst. I feel Jesus. He's grasping for me, reaching out His hand, urging me to finally reach back, to take His hand, walk through this journey with Him, to not push Him aside like I have always done, believing I know better than He does, believing that I don't need Him to be free, to actually believe the scriptures I am reading, feel them down deep, in all the corners of my heart and soul. I want to believe. I need to try something else. What I am doing isn't working. I'm fighting against Him, not with Him. I know what I need to do. I talk to my husband about it first, and after we are both in agreeance, I know it's time to meet with the pastor of the church.

***

We have dinner with him and his wife shortly after one of our first visits to the church. They reach out, wanting to get to know us a little better, and they are one of the first few people that wanted to hear my side of the story. They don't set assumptions and base their opinions on us by what they read and/or heard about us. It's at this dinner that we express our initial fears of going to a church, the judgment and gossip we expect to encounter from bad past experiences, and we aren't sure we can face anymore. It's at this moment that they look at us with so much love, and in such a matter-of-fact way, the pastor says, "If anyone from my church treats you that way, then they don't belong in my church." It's the most powerful statement he can say to us at that moment, and we know he means it. It's that love and acceptance that ensures my husband and me that their church is where we belong.

I show up early to church the following Sunday and ask to speak with him and his wife. I'm so nervous that as soon as we are in the pastor's office, I just blurt it out.

"I want to get baptized. I am giving my life over to Jesus Christ as my Lord and Savior." There, it's over with.

They both look at me; the pastor's wife has tears in her eyes and then so do I.

We discuss all the details, the vision I have for my baptism, and we decide that I will address the congregation for the first time. I'm going to share my testimony, my truth, and finally break free from the chains that bind me, No longer hiding from a past I can't change.

I did it. I have made more bad decisions in my life than I can count, but it's time to embrace them, to turn my test into my testimony and this is the first step.

**

I am baptized in August 2019. There is a video, but since that doesn't help with what we are currently doing, I am going to share my testimony that I read to my congregation right before I am baptized with all of you.

DISCLAIMER: Now, some of this testimony might contain repetitive information that I have shared with you earlier in this book, so if you have no desire to possibly read some bits of information you have heard before, no problem at all. You can simply just skip past it. I am choosing to include my testimony because to me, it's a very important part of the story. It's a big moment for me, and I think there is something so raw about reading what I wrote back then versus how I can discuss it all with you now. Whichever you decide is fine, and I thank you for going on this journey with me.

I was raised Catholic and always felt like I believed there was a God. I did the whole thing: communion, confirmation, Sunday School, and church. When asked if I believed in God of course I said, "Yes." I believed, but we did not have a relationship. Honestly, I didn't give Him much thought.

My childhood was rough. I grew up in an abusive home where everything was unstable and scary, and I felt alone. I was dispensable. My biological father never wanted me; my stepfather was an alcoholic and very abusive; and my mom told me over and over that she would choose him over me every time. She said that was what the Bible said—put your husband first. I don't know if that is true or not, but as a child, it hurt and made me upset with God. He couldn't have wanted this for me.

I ran away from home at seventeen, and God couldn't have felt further away. I had met a boy, and he loved me, accepted me, and wanted to take care of me. His family was my family. It was all I had ever wanted. I was searching for love and acceptance in all the wrong places. God did not have a place in my life.

I began to make choices for those relationships that would alter my life forever. I was able to justify my sin no matter how wrong I knew it was because I didn't want to disappoint them. I needed them to love me. I didn't want to be thrown away. They told me how special I was. That they loved me and counted on me. So, I did things I didn't want to do, and anytime God tried to reach me, I pushed Him away. Their love and acceptance were all I thought I needed.

I eventually left that life, and then on May 17, 2018, my world came crashing down. The consequences of those choices from my past were now threatening my future. I was federally in trouble, and the word *prison* became common in conversation. I sank into a deep depression, and I didn't know how to go on. I was scared and ashamed.

I have a beautiful little girl who is my whole world, and the thought of being taken away from her or not seeing her face every day is unbearable or leaving my husband behind, who has loved me so fearlessly. I was frozen. It was painful to even look at my family some days. It was a horrible seven months of an emotional roller coaster—lost relationships, self-reflection, and not knowing what my future holds. I was trying to do it on my own, and that wasn't working.

On January 1, 2019, I opened my Bible. I had no other choice. When everything was crumbling down and I had nowhere to turn, I looked up. I dove into the Lord's word and fell to my knees more times than I can count. I asked Him to forgive me. Forgive me for my sins, for losing sight of Him, and for not being the person I knew He created me to be. I still don't know what my future holds or what my earthly consequences are going to be, but I know that Jesus loves me and has forgiven me. We are in a relationship, and I know all the love and acceptance I was searching for can only be found in Him.

Finding God has completely changed my life. I am not the same person I was before this. I fully believe that this was the path that God knew I had to take to bring me closer to Him. I now have peace where there was despair and hope where I thought all was lost. I am humbled and truly grateful for all the blessings that God has given me. I am a better mother, wife, friend, and person through God's amazing grace, and I know that I am FORGIVEN!

***

I cry so much while I read this. I didn't think I looked up once. I can't see them—my family and friends—that stuck by us, sitting in the front rows. I'm shaking. I'm afraid of the response, anxious for finally saying the truth out loud. I have lived in hiding for so long, never really letting anyone in, not wanting to be seen for who and what I am. Now, I am laying it all out in front of them to do with what they want. It's the most vulnerable I have ever been.

When I am done, I climb into the water in a t-shirt that was made just for me with the word *Forgiven* written across the front, the pastor on one side and my husband on the other. I plug my nose, and they bend me back. I am only underwater for a couple of seconds, but to me, it feels like a lifetime. I let it wash over every part of me, willing it to take with it all the pain, hurt, and shame I have carried for so long. To rid me of every negative thought that I believed about myself, the lies that I was only the sum of my mistakes, unworthy of forgiveness, of love.

As I am lifted from the water back into the seated position, I feel it all leave my body through the tears that I am uncontrollably shedding.

The pastor begins to speak; he's praying over me, and for the first time in my life, I feel like a child of God. I exit the tub, go to the restroom to change, and then sit with my family while we watch the others accept Jesus Christ into their lives.

I haven't had time to give much thought to my testimony or what it means now that everyone in the church knows. I did it for me, to finally break free of my chains, but it isn't until church is over that I realized it was so much bigger than that.

People start coming up to me, hugging me, encouraging me, and telling me how proud they are that I shared my story. Two moments, in particular, stand out. One's the lady who stops me before I leave to let me know how much my words impacted her. She has a son who is incarcerated and searching for hope, something to believe in, and she asks if she can mail him a copy of my testimony. I'm floored. It's an incredible honor, so of course I say yes.

The second is the man that approaches me as my family, and I open the doors to leave. He is an older man, one that honestly, I haven't noticed before, but that comes as no surprise as before I was hiding, not trying to meet people, not interested in making friends. I notice as he hugs me that his eyes were glossed over, like he's been crying.

He says to me, "My dear girl, if you would have taken the time to look up as you were reading, you would have seen that we were all crying with you." His words hit me like a truck. I immediately start crying again, and we hug. He tells me how he never cries; he isn't the crying type, but my story has touched him. He's so happy that I shared it.

***

It makes me want to tear up now all this time later when I think back on it. I can't believe that someone had such a nice thing to say to me. That my story would affect somebody in any way, let alone bring them to tears. I was truly touched, and I knew it was God beginning to use me for His glory. I wish I could tell you that after that everything was great, and I was changed, happy, and positive all the time, but that isn't real life.

***

We continue reading our Bible. We have a goal, and the year is fast approaching. As my husband and I start to delve deeper into our faith, we begin to get more involved in church. We help where we can and even join a Bible study. But, despite our growing faith, the truth is, hard things are still hard. Blind faith and trust are incredibly difficult for me. Trusting something I can't physically see, or touch is a challenge. I struggle, waver, and remind myself that I am only human. I have bad days, where I fall back into my old mindset, where things seem impossibly hard, and hopelessness takes over.

Getting baptized doesn't make the waiting any easier. The war Satan is raging on me feels like it intensified. It's like Satan's mad he lost one and is coming after me with everything he has. But even on those hard days, I remind myself of the hope and love I have found through God.

God is healing my brokenness, including the relationships in my life. One of the most important relationships is the one transforming between my mother and me.

Our journey toward faith started in her kitchen on that heart-wrenching Christmas trip. Together, we want to grow, to leave behind the way we have been living for so many years. We crave hope, love, and faith and want to experience all the goodness the Lord has to offer.

The journey with my mother is not easy. It requires forgiveness and grace from both of us, but it is worth it. My relationship with my mother now is amazing. She is my best friend, and we work every day to be the people God calls us to be. She inspires me and radiates God's grace in every aspect of her life.

We are not perfect, but the beauty of it is, God doesn't call us to be perfect, He calls us to be faithful. Our faithfulness is what pleases Him. We are all flawed and make mistakes, but it is our commitment to God and our willingness to follow Him that matters most. God knows that we are not perfect, but He loves us anyway and desires a personal relationship with each of us. He calls us to trust in Him, seek His guidance, and to walk in obedience to His will. When we stumble, He is there to pick us up, and when we succeed, He is there to celebrate with us. So let us strive for faithfulness and let our love for God be the foundation of our lives. God is a healer, the way maker, and I tell you, friends, if God can do it for me, I know He can do it for you too.

Remember, mending broken relationships requires trust in Him, prayer, and small steps toward healing. But His love can overcome any hurt or pain, and His healing power can transform any broken relationship.

The love that comes from mending my relationships is immeasurable. The thought of being away from my family is unbearable. I am so proud of where we are going on our journey that the thought of being removed from it all seems impossible. I can't imagine missing my daughter growing up, not being there for her birthdays, and being ripped away from my husband in his biggest time of need. I am afraid of losing the traction I am growing every day with my mother, of missing out on our daily phone calls and how she always knew the right thing to say at the right time. I know God is calling me to trust Him, to trust the journey He will have me embark on. Whatever is going to happen is His will, His way, and I need to trust in that with my faith.

Chapter Sixteen

Present

As my sentencing day approaches, I find myself needing to draw out the dark noise in my head, to change the narrative of my thoughts. It's suggested to me that I should listen to the Bible app while I try to go to sleep. You can set a timer for any amount of time you wish, and then, at least, you are falling asleep to God's word versus your own ugly thoughts. I begin to do this at night, and that is when I hear Psalms 13:1-6.

How long, LORD? Will you forget me forever? How long will you hide your face from me? How long must I wrestle with my thoughts and day after day have sorrow in my heart? How long will my enemy triumph over me? Look on me and answer, LORD my God. Give light to my eyes, or I will sleep in death, and my enemy will say, "I have overcome him," and my foes will rejoice when I fall. But I trust in your unfailing love; my heart rejoices in your salvation. I will sing the LORD's praise, for he has been good to me.

I end up falling asleep to this scripture every night, and it helps me quiet all the noise in my head. I try to stay busy during the day, but having to wait to find out my sentencing day is agonizing. The fear and pressure of the outcome lingers over my head; it's been pushed back and rescheduled so many times, and now, I am waiting to hear if they are going to agree to continue it until after the Christmas holiday, so I can be with my family.

Finally, I get word. They have agreed, and my sentencing is scheduled for January 8, 2020. That's it; it's set. I now know the day my fate will be decided. Now that I know, I am starting to think that not knowing is better. Now, every day is a countdown.

My attorney tells me that I need to write a letter to the judge, a personal narrative that will help him get to know and possibly understand me better and at sentencing hopefully show me some mercy. My attorney also suggests that I find as many people as I can to write support letters to the judge on my behalf. That seems almost as hard as the personal narrative because I only have one friend that stuck by me through my old life and still knows me now. I decided I'll ask her, and for the others, I'll pick people to testify to the changes I have made and focus more on the life I am living now versus who I was before. Thankfully, each person I ask this favor of says yes, and so I have four letters that will be coming. The personal narrative and the letters of character, let's call them, have to be mailed to the judge at the courthouse a month before sentencing.

Here is the letter I wrote the judge:

Dear Judge,

This is the hardest letter I have ever written. I appreciate you taking the time to read it. I have the utmost respect for you and your time, so I have been going over this repeatedly to try and get my point across as quickly as possible. I have completely and utterly messed up. I am so disappointed in myself and the decisions I have made. There is no justification or reason I can give except most of my life I have been broken. I grew up in an unstable, abusive environment. I've been thrown away and pushed aside most of my childhood. I didn't know that unconditional love existed. At the age of 17, I ran away from home. I had met a boy on vacation in Las Vegas, Nevada while visiting my aunt. He swept me off my feet and promised to take care of me and he loved me. As I write that I realize how pathetic that sounds. I was so weak, seeking love and approval from anyone that I allowed myself to make choices to do things I knew were wrong, illegal, and completely ridiculous to feel loved/needed/important. I didn't know what I would do if he didn't want me anymore or how he would get mad at me every time I would say no. I am not excusing any of it and I now know there is no one to blame in this situation but me. I made my choice; I justified it and I take full responsibility for the role that I played. I believed that I wasn't hurting anyone. I believed people when they told me it was fine, it's business, and they'll write it off as a loss and get their money back. No big deal. I was so wrong. I never thought about the big picture. The businesses being hurt, the people that worked there, the amazing EMTs, firemen, and police officers that cared for me. I know that Insurance Fraud is not a victimless crime, and I am so sorry from the bottom of my heart for my involvement in such an activity. I was caring for my daughter last night and as I was staring at her I was thinking about how I have let her down. The shame and guilt that I have inside me are overwhelming. The childhood I so badly wanted her to have, how I always wanted her to know how loved she is, how blessed I have been that God chose me to be her mother, are all being negated by my poor decisions from the exact opposite that I wanted for her. Now there is a chance that I have hurt my daughter in the worst possible way by having to leave her without me. The pain of that is something I pray every day I can somehow forgive myself for. This experience has completely changed me. The last year and a half have brought so much growth, faith, and change for me that in some instances I see it as a blessing. The Lord has a way of knocking you on the head when He tries to get your attention and you're too stubborn to listen. The person I wanted to be was so far from the person I was. I was seeking love, acceptance, and my worth from all the wrong places. I knew who God was, but I didn't have a relationship with Him. I didn't know that in Him you could find strength, hope, and love as you've never known. That on that path I would never be fulfilled. I would never be the mother my daughter deserved or the wife my husband needed. Not when I wasn't right with myself. After becoming friends with a neighbor who is now someone very important to me and her seeing how lost I truly was she encouraged me to read the Bible. I got on my hands and knees and prayed to God to save me. To be the woman He created me to be and who I truly believed in my heart I was. I would also a few weeks later end up in a church that I now call home. What a life-changing friend. I am hesitant to share this with you because I don't want it to sound cliché or an unbelieving (great you found God; they all do) kind of thing. It has just so completely saved me that I don't know how to not share it or to give all the credit to God and His amazing Grace, Love, and Forgiveness. It has been a year and a half of hard truths, pain, tears, and prayers. I committed myself fully to my new way of life and was baptized on August 11, 2019. I started receiving therapy to tackle my issues so I would never repeat my mistakes and could learn how to no longer seek my worth from others. I am a child of God and everything I have ever needed can only be found through Him. In dealing with the repercussions of my past life I don't even recognize that person and can't believe she was me. I have asked for forgiveness from my Lord and Savior, from my family, and my church, and I ask the same of you. I was once isolated and now I have an amazing support system that holds me accountable every day. I have an amazing husband and daughter, and nothing is ever worth me hurting them this way again. I help run our family business; I homeschool our daughter and plan on teaching her everything I now know that I was never taught about God, caring for us, and most importantly the value of who you are. I have opened myself up to friendships and have let people see me and get to know me, we pray together and go to Bible studies together twice a week. I am part of my community, volunteering, and planning events for the church. I want to talk to at-risk teens about the repercussions of the choices they make, and how important it is to love yourself, to be brave, and to stand up for right and wrong. My story has already inspired multiple people at my church, and I just hope to be able to continue that and touch the lives of as many people as I can. Again, I am so sorry for the role that I played in this situation that has taken up so much of your time and the time of everyone else that is forced to be here to have to deal with it. I believe that whatever punishment you feel is necessary for me to receive will be fair and just and I will accept that fate gracefully and promise that we shall never meet this way again.

Respectfully,

Brittany Cecilia Jo

This is honestly one of the hardest letters I have ever had to write. I send it off to my attorney, and he forwards it to the judge. I will know the outcome soon enough.

The holidays come, and we try to find joy in the moments, appreciating the little time that we have left.

I will be honest and tell you, I struggle immensely. I know that I am powerless. There is nothing I can do to change the circumstance, but it doesn't make it any easier.

I cry every day as I begin to prepare for my sentencing. I buy my daughter a stuffed bear for Christmas that has a Bluetooth speaker in it that links to my phone where I can record messages and songs to her that will play through the bear. I record all of the nighttime songs we sing, and the prayer we say every night. I record birthday messages where I sing "Happy Birthday" to her for each birthday I think I might miss. It takes me hours to get through them as I cry harder and harder with each song, picturing her face and knowing that I am going to be away from her, and it guts me. I print pictures for her to have and ones I want to be mailed to me when I arrive at whatever prison I will be going to.

New Year's Eve comes, and once again, I find it impossible to be excited about anything the new year will bring. I already know what it is going to bring me—prison time.

We have friends over and try to make the most of it, but as the countdown begins, with every tick of another second down, I know I am that much closer to my life turning completely upside down. When midnight comes, all I feel is dread, and as I watch the people around me toast and cheer, I can no longer hold back the tears that have been burning my eyes, aching for release all evening. They break free, and all I can do is succumb to the grief as it overtakes my body. My friends cry with me.

The next week seems to fly by but also drag on forever. I try to remain present in the moments, and friends and family stop by to say their goodbyes, as I am told if I do indeed end up being sentenced to prison, they will take me into custody immediately.

Our final church service is filled with tears and prayer. The pastor brings me down to the front of the congregation and puts his hands on me as he prays, my head bowed, the weight of my future barreling down on me becoming too much to carry, and I sink down to my knees.

One by one, I begin to feel more hands on me, more voices praying over me. I slowly raise my head, and through the haze of my tears see forty or fifty people surrounding me, all with their hands laid on the person in front of them, creating this surge of energy, a powerful chain that led straight to me. It is one of the most beautiful sights I have ever seen, and it becomes deeply engraved in my mind. These are my people, my family, and I know no matter what my husband and my daughter are going to be okay because they have all of them to lean on.

My daughter can feel a shift in energy and knows that something is wrong, but she doesn't know what. I do my best to protect her from the pain, hoping that she is young enough that she won't remember the chunk of time mommy is gone. I hug her more often and hold her tight a little longer. I kiss my husband each time like it is my last, leaving no doubt in his mind about how truly loved he is.

Looking back, I realize that those final days leading up to my sentencing are truly how we all should be living our lives every day. You never know when that moment will be the last with that friend, when that hug or kiss goodnight with your child will be the last, when your last *I love you* will be spoken to the love of your life. It is so important to remember that we are not promised anything on this earth. We never know when the last time is going to be last time, and when that moment comes, will you be able to know in your heart that you left nothing on the table, or will you be filled with regret? I don't want there to be anything left on my table.

The night before I am to be sentenced, sleep evades me, and I lie quietly in my bed, listening to my husband breathe, memorizing the sounds so I can log them into my memory. I then creep out of bed and enter my daughter's room. For multiple reasons, we'll be leaving for court before she wakes up, and these are my last few moments with her. I watch her sleep; her face is so peaceful; it causes me agonizing pain to know this will be the last time I might see her for a very long time. It kills me that she will be suffering from not having her mother, and there's no one to blame besides myself.

I don't know how much of a heart I have left, knowing each day it's been shattered into a million pieces. What can be left? How much can one heart take? I pray over and over again, asking God to comfort her, watch out for her, and everyday place it on her mind how much I love her. As I exit her room, I look back one last time, one last look at my whole world, and then close the door behind me.

We ride to the courthouse with some of our friends, my nerves getting the best of me and my stomach. I am a mess. I can't eat or drink anything. I will myself to have some coffee because, let's be honest, I'm not sure when the next time I will have a good cup of coffee is going to be.

After about an hour, we arrive at the courthouse. I exit the car, my legs feeling like Jell-O. I feel my husband's hand wrap into mine as he presses the side of his body against me, allowing my weight to rest against his. I take a minute to soak in the moment. His face stares so lovingly at me as the glistening of tears shows in his eyes. My friends are not as strong. Their tears form pools of liquid in their eyes.

I am petrified of what was about to happen and, at the same time, am so filled with love for the people standing there with me. The ones who have supported me, laughed with me, and cried thousands of tears with me. The moment has come. Almost two years after this nightmare began, I am about to find out my fate.

We enter the courthouse, process through the metal detector, and then enter the elevator that will bring me to my judgment. As we exit the elevator, I am halted abruptly by the crowd of people gathering outside the courtroom doors. There is no way for me to hide the surprise and utter joy that I feel in my heart as I realize they are there for me. All my church family that has rallied behind us this past year, cried with us, prayed with us, and supported us are now all standing there, waiting to walk into the courtroom with me. A huge sign of support not only to me but for the judge to see as well. I am not alone. The girl who once lived her life in the shadows, afraid to let others in, the girl who had to hide what she was, and the things she had done is now gone. This girl is loved; this girl owns her mistakes and is better for it. This girl is me.

I enter the courtroom, my head held high, as I walk over to my attorney. My husband and all of our friends fill up almost every pew there is available. I am humbled, and my attorney is impressed. We sit down on our side of the small room, and I find myself having to close my eyes and steady my breathing. I try my best to calm the anxiety that is now my constant companion.

The courtroom assistant walks in, her voice commanding the room. "All rise."

The judge is entering; this is it. I begin to pray.

God, I come to you today with a heavy heart and a spirit that is weighed down by the challenges I have brought on myself. I am in desperate need of Your help and guidance, as I face a situation that seems to have no hope. I pray for a positive outcome, even though I know the odds are against me. I ask for the strength and courage to face this challenge and whatever challenges may come next. Please give me the patience to wait for Your divine intervention and the faith to trust in Your plan, even when it doesn't make sense to me. I know that You are a God of miracles, and I believe that You are able to do the impossible. I ask that You show me Your mercy and grace, that You would provide whatever I will need to get through this difficult time. I know that Your ways are greater than mine. Your plans are bigger than my plans, and I know that Your will be done.

I give You all the praise and honor, and I trust in Your love and goodness. Thank You for all that You have done for me and for being with me through this storm. In Jesus's name, Amen.

I feel a peace that I know can only come from God. I am not in control of the situation or the outcome. Whatever is going to happen is supposed to happen. I sit and wait.

The two opposing sides go back and forth, stating their arguments, why they feel they are right, and what their recommendation is for my punishment. Finally, at last, it is the judge's turn to render his decision. I stand, placing my hands on the table in front of me for support. My knees are weak, giving a little more every second, threatening to send me straight to the ground. I face the judge. This is it. I fight the burning of my eyes, forcing the tears to stay away. I don't want to cry, not at this moment.

The judge begins to speak, and he acknowledges the crowd in the room and believes that I have changed, even stating that he fully expects to never see me in his courtroom again. I begin to feel hopeful, maybe he had seen, maybe this would go another way. It's when he said the word "however" that I know my hope is lost. However, I have to pay for my crime. He can't just slap me on the wrist and send me on my way, too many people are watching. What will it say to someone that might attempt to do the same thing we did, that it is a punish less crime? He can't have that. The following few moments go something like this: "Brittany Cecilia Jo, I am hereby sentencing you to thirteen months imprisonment, followed by three years of supervision. You will also have restitution to pay back to your victims. Your attorney has requested you be able to self-surrender at the place and time dictated by the Bureau of Prisons, and that request is granted. I see no reason why you can't go home and wait for your instructions. I wish you well, Brittany Cecilia Jo. The court is dismissed." *BANG!*

Just like that, it's done. My mind races. It's a lot of information to absorb. Thirteen months, not as bad as it can be, I realize, but to me, it still feels tragic. A year, a whole year away from my family. It sounds impossible, and the one thing I do not expect is that I am going home. My attorney never told me he asked for the exception and never said there was a possibility I could go back home for a while.

If I am being honest, of course, I am happy to be going back, but I am not looking forward to having to endure the heartbreak of saying goodbye all over again. My attorney walks over to my friends and family, giving them words of encouragement and that the amount of time served wouldn't really be thirteen months. I most likely will be home in ten months on good behavior. That gives us all hope and sets my goal for being home by next Christmas. I don't want to miss Christmas; it's my favorite time of year, and I can't imagine being away from my family during that time.

We all load back up in the car and head home, a drive that I did not envision getting to be a part of. When we arrive home, I run in and hug my daughter as tight as I can. She thinks I am being silly, never realizing how close she came to not seeing me again that day. I am on borrowed time, and I'm not going to waste it. I know now what's coming, what we are all going to have to endure. It becomes another waiting game. Now, I know I am going to prison; I just have to wait to figure out where they are going to send me.

I have researched women's federal prisons a few months earlier and saw that there was one in Seattle and a few in California. I researched them all, and it seems Dublin California is the one to hope for. It has gotten a lot of coverage when Felicity Huffman served her short prison sentence there in October of 2019.

It seems so surreal that this is my life now. I am picking out which prison I want to go to like I am choosing my next vacation destination. I have no idea how I am going to do this. I focus on just being present and cherish every day with my family and friends, thankful to have been given this extra time with them. If I would have been taken into custody right away, I would have sat in the county jail until my report date to prison and then would have been transported by the authorities. I know I don't want to be in county jail. That extra time is a show of grace and misery from Jesus; I have no doubt.

A couple of days after my sentencing, we have one of our biggest snowstorms of the year. We play outside as a family, make snowmen, and have a snowball fight. That day is the day I take one of my favorite pictures of my daughter, and it becomes one of the pictures I take with me.

One day, as we're painting each other's nails, my daughter looks at me and says, "Mom, this is so satisfying."

I can't help but laugh, but I also notice the pull on my heart. I realize that I have been so caught up in my own pain, my own anguish, battling the demons inside of me, that I have allowed myself to be only half in my life for two years. Two years that she didn't get everything she should have from me. Why am I not treasuring our time together every day? Why does it take a tragic circumstance for me to realize what is important? To cherish my family the way I always should have.

A couple of weeks later, my letter from the Bureau of Prisons arrived, and I am to report to FCI Dublin on February 20, 2020 by noon. As soon as the decision is made, I waste no time buying our airline tickets to California. It's a weird feeling, unlike the excitement that most people feel when they book a ticket to California. I only feel dread.

I dive headfirst into research, studying everything I can about the prison, its address, mail procedures, and commissary. Most importantly, I research to see if anyone from my case will also be there. I look up name after name and that's when I see it. Richard's sister is there. I am immediately filled with dread. We had always gotten along when Richard and I were together, but when we broke up, she sent me a nasty email, calling me various names. One, in particular, suggested that I was a gold-digger, and I was basically trash. She also mentioned that if she ever saw me again, she was going to, well putting it nicely, kick my butt. Great, just what I need. I'm already worried about how I am going to handle the other women in the prison, and now I have to worry about her too.

All the planning and research gives me a false sense of control. I need to feel like I am in control of something, and being as prepared as possible is the only way I think to do it. After I have planned as much as I can, we focus on each day and anything we want to accomplish together before I leave.

We reach our goal of reading the entire Bible the day before my sentencing, and all I can say is, you cannot read the Bible and not be changed. We go back to our church, knowing we need their love and support now more than ever. Everyone is as surprised to see me, as I am to be there. They offer us hope, love, and an abundance of prayer.

With each passing day, my surrender date approaches, and the weight of leaving my family behind grows heavier. Battling Satan's lies in my head becomes an everyday occurrence, and some days, his voice is so loud that it's all I can hear. But even during the toughest moments, I cling to God's promise. In Isaiah 43:1, he states, "*Do not fear, for I have redeemed you; I have summoned you by name; you are mine. When you pass through the waters, I will be with you; and when you pass through the rivers, they will not sweep over you. When you walk through the fire, you will not be burned; the flames will not set you ablaze.*"

I engrave these words on my heart, knowing that this promise is what I need to take with me. The day finally arrives, and it's time to leave, this time for good. I cry all the tears my body has to give and holds my sweet baby girl, letting her know I will be gone for a little while, but I'll be back. I choose to tell her I am going to school, a place where I can learn and better myself, not a whole lie. I know the person that goes into that prison will not be the same person that comes out. I tell her once I get settled, she can come to visit me there soon.

My husband and I leave for the airport, the weight of the world on both of our shoulders. The car ride is a somber one. I'm plagued with fear, worry, and anxiety about what is to come, and my husband is carrying the burden that very soon he will be the only parent at home. The thought of juggling work, home, and life balance alone is daunting, even for the best of us. I wish I could take it all back and make everything better for them both, but I can't. I look out the window, watching as the trees pass swiftly by as we drive down the road. I can't find any words to say; there's nothing I can say that will bring comfort or make this situation any better. It seems foolish to even try, so instead, we ride the rest of the way in silence.

We arrive at the airport, and since it's going to be a quick trip for my husband, at least, we choose to just leave the car for him in the parking garage. It feels weird traveling with no luggage. I don't need it.

We arrive at our gate, and now, all we have to do is wait. I take a photo of our plane as we are getting ready to board, with the sun rising right behind its wings. When I see the beauty of it, I feel hope. I decide to post the picture on social media; in a way, I'm communicating that we are here, we're doing this.

Next to the picture, I post a scripture from Jeremiah 29:11. *"For I know the plans I have for you," declares the Lord, "Plans to prosper you and not to harm you, plans to give you hope and a future."*

If there's anything I can give you from this whole book, I pray that it is hope. Hope feeds your soul, fills you with purpose, and gives you the strength to carry on, even in the most difficult of circumstances. Without hope, I'm afraid we would all perish.

The plane ride is uneventful, a quick two-and-a-half-hour ride from Washington. We land in Oakland, California on February 19, 2020, the day before I am to turn myself in. We check into our hotel room and decide to soak up every last moment that we have together. It's hard to try and find joy in the moments. I don't want to take them for granted, but we find it challenging as we are fighting the intense grief we're feeling. We do our best, though, and thankfully find ourselves in moments of laughter, moments of love and moments of peace.

He's my best friend, and nobody can make me laugh more than he can. I feel whole when I'm with him. He affects me like no one else, and it's our love that's going to get us through this. Well, that and a whole lot of Jesus.

We decide to leave the room, get some fresh air, and be present in the day we have with each other. We walk around town, taking in the sights, and decide we'll go have lunch. It's when we arrive for lunch that

I realize I lost my driver's license; it has fallen out of my pocket somewhere along the way. Panic sets in. This is a disaster. One of the main requirements for my surrender is that I need to bring my license with me, and they will be keeping it until my release. I'm not sure why besides verifying I am who I am supposed to be.

We retrace our steps all the way back toward the hotel, and by the grace of God, it's lying there on the sidewalk. There's my face, staring right back at me. I found it. There are tons of people walking around, but not one person took it. It's a miracle.

Relieved to have my license back, we head back to the restaurant to have lunch. By this point, we're able to laugh about it, but for a while, no one is laughing. After lunch, we go back to the hotel and talk about what our life will be like when I return home, try to be positive, and make plans for things we can look forward to. We call our friends and family so I can tell them I love them one more time, and they pray with me. I call my daughter and talk to her about her ballet class, and she tells me how much fun she's having with her sister. It makes me smile to know she's having such a great day. We go to one of my favorite restaurants for dinner, P.F. Chang's, to have my final good meal, at least for a while. We eat until I can't possibly take another bite and enjoy a bottle of champagne. If the situation wasn't so dreadful, it would have been a perfect evening.

Later that night, lying in bed, I once again let the sorrow take over me. I have no idea how I am going to do this; how am I going to leave them? My heart aches in a way it has never ached before. I don't sleep much that night. The next morning is the day I have been dreading— the day I have to turn myself in.

We pack up our things and leave the hotel early. We still have a couple of hours before I need to be at the prison, so we stop at a restaurant that's close to it and have some breakfast. I, of course, can't eat. I have no appetite, and my stomach is in such knots I probably wouldn't have been able to keep anything down anyway. I keep watching the clock, watching the minutes tick by, inching closer and closer to noon. I have never yearned for time to stop more than I did right then. Unfortunately, to my dismay, it doesn't, and sooner than I would have liked, it's time to head to the prison.

Driving in silence, the absence of noise only amplifies the deafening weight of my thoughts. We arrive a little early, so we sit in the car for a while, neither of us wanting to be the first to get out. Finally, we both muster the courage to exit the car and head to the entrance. I can't fully describe the feeling I have as I walk through the doors of the prison. It's a mix of fear, sadness, and disbelief. I'm scared out of my mind, and I don't know what to expect.

The front area is a cold room surrounded by windows, and there's a desk that sits along the back wall where an officer is sitting, and it has a table next to it. There are about six or seven chairs lining the other wall and behind the desk is a hallway that goes in three different directions. I can't help but wonder which direction I will be taken once I am processed.

I check in with the officer sitting behind the desk, and he instructs my husband and me to take a seat. I have done research on items you were allowed to bring in with you, so I am completely shattered when he tells me I can't wear my silicone wedding ring or my cross, each item that I bought specifically based on their requirements to be able to enter with. I think it's best not to begin this journey by arguing with the officer even though I know he is wrong. I do as he instructs and hand my jewelry to my husband. My body immediately reacts to the emptiness of my missing wedding band, and I want to cry again. We walk over to the chairs that line the wall and wait. My husband tries to comfort me about my jewelry, even putting my wedding band on his ring finger where he says he will wear both of them together until I return home. That's the kind of guy he is.

I read that the wait time for someone to come and process you can be pretty long, so I am shocked when only a short time later they say they're ready for me and that my husband has to leave. I'm not ready; it's too soon. I will never be ready. I squeeze him with every ounce of power I have. As we say goodbye, tears stream down both of our faces, I can't help but feel grateful for the extra time we have together, but selfishly, I want more. A female officer comes out, and I know I am out of time. I kiss my husband one last time, whisper in his ear I love him, and then watch him walk out the door without me. I stare at him, waiting for him to look back. I know he will, and when he does, I give him the biggest smile I can muster and then turn away.

Two years of pain, heartache, and fear all leads to this moment. This is it, the last hurdle to get over to be able to fully move on from the worst thing in my life. It's time for me to pay for the things I did.

As I walk toward the officer that is waiting for me, I know that I'm not going in alone, that God is with me every step of the way. Isaiah 43:1 ran through my mind again. *"Do not fear, for I have redeemed you; I have summoned you by name; you are mine. When you pass through the waters, I will be with you; and when you pass through the rivers, they will not sweep over you. When you walk through the fire, you will not be burned; the flames will not set you ablaze."*

I am seconds away from walking through the fire, and I have to have faith that whatever is to come, God will be with me and set my path straight. This is His plan for me, and I need to do the best I can to make it through.

I walk through the metal detector and am then escorted to a large metal door that lets out the loudest buzzing noise I have ever heard right before it opens, a deafening sound that echoes through the halls and reverberates in my soul. I walk through the door, and the female officer, in an aggressive tone, says, "Back against the wall, inmate."

I am an inmate now, no longer the person I was even just ten minutes ago. The door slams shut. The loud thud of it closing and locking behind me makes me flinch. The fear is growing, and I can feel it building inside my body, consuming every orifice it can find. I know my life is about to change forever, but little do I know just how much. The slamming of that door is just the beginning.

Thank you so much for reading, "BROKEN" your love, encouragement, and support have meant the absolute world to me and I am forever grateful for all of you.

Please enjoy this preview of the second part of my journey coming soon……

As I was led into the dimly lit hallway, a surge of overwhelming fear gripped me tightly, my stomach churning with each hesitant step. I desperately pleaded with my body to hold itself together, to withstand the tornado of emotions threatening to consume me. The hallway, confined and suffocating, bore witness to my entrapment, with doors lurking at both ends. Behind me lay the door I had just passed through, closing off my freedom forever. And ahead of me loomed a door that I knew, with an unsettling certainty, would lead me straight into the depths of my own personal hell.

I fought to shake off the shackles of fear, searching for an inner strength buried deep within. But before I could gather my thoughts, a sudden eruption of shouting shattered the uneasy silence.

"Against the wall, inmate!" barked the officer, her command piercing the air.

My heart raced as I turned to face her, only to realize with a jolt that her words were directed at me. With trembling compliance, I pressed myself as tightly as possible against the unforgiving wall, hoping that somehow it would offer solace, swallowing me into it as a means of escape from this prison of despair.

This was the grim reality that awaited me, a reality from which there was no escape. I knew in that moment that I never wanted to find myself on the wrong side of an officer, especially not within the first ten minutes of my arrival.

As I stood there, questions swirled in my mind, each one a haunting echo of my fears. What lay beyond that ominous door? What horrors awaited me? And most importantly, how could I summon the strength to endure? I closed my eyes, seeking solace in prayer, fervently asking for the divine intervention that would grant me the resilience I so desperately needed.

"Dear God, grant me the strength to navigate this treacherous path. Watch over me, guide me, and shield me from the perils that lie ahead. With Your unwavering presence, I can overcome any obstacle. I feel Your presence, Lord."

With newfound resolve, I opened my eyes, inhaling deeply, filling my lungs with determination. I was ready to face whatever awaited beyond that threshold. Taking a courageous step forward, I followed the officer as she led me through the door, only to be greeted by the scorching sun outside.

We traveled down a short sidewalk, leading us to another building. As we approached a door, the piercing buzz filled my ears once more, signaling our entry. Stepping into yet another confined hallway, the officer's voice barked the familiar command.

"Against the wall, inmate."

This time, I reacted swiftly, my senses on high alert, my mind prepared for the unexpected. Another deafening buzz resonated as the door ahead swung open. I followed the female officer through the threshold and found myself in a room divided into two separate cells. Each cell teemed with fellow inmates, some donning green uniforms while others wore tan.

I recalled the information my attorney had shared—green for the camp, where I fervently hoped to find myself, and tan for the higher security prison adjacent to it. A male officer sat behind the desk we now approached, his gaze scrutinizing me, filling me with unease. But then, surprisingly, a smile graced his lips.

"What's your name?" he inquired.

Before I could respond, the female officer intervened, curtly interjecting, "This is 21220-085."

In that moment, I realized I was reduced to nothing more than a number, this was my life now.